Is it Cricket?

By the same author
ARCHIE: A Biography of A.C. MacLaren

POWER, MONEY & POLITICS IN CRICKET SINCE 1945

Is it Cricket?

MICHAEL DOWN

Queen Anne Press

For James and Geoffrey

A *Queen Anne Press* BOOK

© Michael G. Down 1985

First published in Great Britain in 1985
by Queen Anne Press,
Macdonald & Co (Publishers) Ltd,
Maxwell House, 74 Worship Street,
London EC2A 2EN

A BPCC plc company

British Library Cataloguing in Publication Data
Is It Cricket?
  1. Cricket-History
  1. Title
  796.35'8'09   GV913

   ISBN 0-356-10799-X

Typeset by Cylinder Typesetting Ltd, London
Printed and bound in Great Britain by
Biddles Ltd, Guildford and King's Lynn

Contents

Preface

It was Sir Norman Birkett who observed that any writer who attempts to add a new cricket book to the game's already over-flowing bibliography is bound 'by a kind of literary justice to inform his readers distinctly and specifically what it is he professes to supply and what he expects to improve'. With such a warning in mind it can be stated clearly that this book is essentially a study of first-class cricket as played in Britain since the end of the last war. No attempt has been made to duplicate the many fine histories of this period that have been published previously; this is not a book of match descriptions or scores or player biography – all these can be found elsewhere. Instead, a new approach is taken with the emphasis on social history or, to be more precise, on cricket's own social history. Hopefully, sufficient new and interesting ground will be covered to pass Sir Norman's legal scrutiny.

As this is written, we are approaching the fortieth post-war cricket season and it is increasingly apparent that the game has undergone massive and irreversible change since the carefree days of Compton and Edrich, of Hutton, Bedser and Evans. That era of the late forties and early fifties seems far removed from the big business of today's highly paid stars, one day games, sponsorship deals and endless controversies. In common with other major sports, cricket has become a highly commercial, intensively marketed enterprise and the 'Americanization' of the game is well in hand. While traditionalists may bemoan this trend, nostalgic memories of the early post-war boom cannot hide the fact that by the end of the fifties county cricket was all but dying on its feet. This phenomenon, and the modern resuscitation of cricket, forms the heart of this study. The social forces at work and the price cricket has paid for its survival are the key ingredients. It has been argued that cricket cannot be isolated from events in the broader sphere, and as the everyday life of Britain has undergone overwhelming change in the post-war period, so professional sport – in particular cricket – has changed in response.

The main body of this book concerns itself with the dramatic changes in cricket during the years 1946 to 1963. The latter was a pivotal season that saw the birth of the Gillette Cup, the demise of the 'Gentleman' (in name and occasionally behaviour) and the emergence of the West Indies as the dominating force in modern cricket. It is hoped that these events and other trends can best be rationalized by tracing their history from cricket's earliest times right through to the present day. As the story unfolds so the inevitability of today's controversies becomes apparent. From South Africa to Packer, from betting and drug scandals to the Boycott row, they are all part of cricket's social history.

As to acknowledgements, a number of people have helped considerably in the preparation of this work and their efforts are greatly appreciated. In particular, Jim Coldham (who read the entire manuscript and offered many improvements and valuable discussion), John Newth, Sir Leonard Hutton, Geoffrey Edrich, Frank Tyson and Michael Stewart contributed in various ways. Linda McGrath prepared the typescript in faultless fashion. As far as written sources are concerned, the most important are listed in the bibliography. Of these, perhaps *The Times* newspaper was referred to most often, not, as Enoch Powell once suggested, because 'it really is such a museum of obsolescent attitudes as to be impossible to avoid quoting' but mainly by virtue of its fine index. The most important credits, however, must go to Bill Neill-Hall for seeing the book into print, and to my wife, Margaret, for constant encouragement, understanding and advice.

Finally, having spent so many hours with pen in hand, the following lines written by E. V. Lucas in 1898 seem strangely appropriate:

> More mighty than the bat, the pen,
>   And mightier still as we grow old,
> And hence I needs must scribble when
>   I'd fain be bowling – or be bowled.
> Yet thoughts, whate'er the task, will stray,
>   To work they never wholly yield;
> And mine, on every sunny day,
>   Are in the field, are in the field!

1
Cricket and Contemporary Life

Cricket through the ages has been well served by its historians, ranging in style from the romantic Pycroft to the statistical Haygarth; from the controversial Bowen to the definitive Altham. While these and other historians can provide us with a wealth of detail concerning matches, series, players, records, laws and the like, they have given less room to the relationship between cricket and the society in which it is played. In recent times, it is true, there have been many learned treatises on the general subject of sport and its role in the everyday life of the people, but these works have often been the product of detailed sociological research and are typically couched in academic language. Indeed, they frequently have a political axe to grind or a socio-economic theory to prove and, as such, are of limited use to the average sports enthusiast. Cricket has itself been the subject of more popular thesis-style treatment along sociological lines, notably by Ford (*Cricket: A Social History 1700-1835*, David & Charles, 1972) and Brookes (*English Cricket: The Game and its Players through the Ages*, Weidenfeld & Nicolson, 1978). Cricket surely deserves this specialized treatment since, more than almost any other sport in England, it is woven deep into the fabric of society, its influence embracing the most noble-born and the most humble. In fact, this bridging of all strata within British society makes it an ideal subject for analysis and discussion. Ford summarizes this idea as follows: 'It is my belief that any sport has the seeds of its development planted within the soil of social custom. It can only be properly understood and described if the social influences contemporaneous with its development are studied and related to the peculiar development of the sport.'

Another perspective on this theme of 'cricket in society', and one perhaps more agreeable to many cricket enthusiasts, is that given by the romantic school of writers. Foremost under this heading must always come Sir Neville Cardus, in whose work cumbersome academic apparatus and sociological theorizing are replaced by an intrinsic feeling for the place of cricket in society. The result has been literature of the very highest standard. The single most important theme in his writings was always the notion that in cricket an individual's character was truly revealed. His beloved Emmott Robinson, Archie MacLaren or Ted Wainwright were made the subjects of anecdotes to demonstrate this point time after time. On occasion, though, Cardus went further in suggesting that a nation's collective character was portrayed in the way the game was played at any time in history. In 1934 he wrote, 'English cricket has usually reflected the social scene or psychology of the country at large in any given period.' Again, in 1945, 'Cricket somehow holds up a mirror to the English nature.'

This basic thesis was taken up and expanded by the man who, without being an imitator of Cardus, has certainly been more than worthy of following in his footsteps – John Arlott. Tempering Cardus' pure romanticism with a more factual approach and a deep feeling for the idea that a study of cricket was essentially a study of people, Arlott has written, 'Perhaps the most convincing proof of the fact that cricket is of wider importance than its standing as a sport qua sport, is its invariably faithful reflection of its regional and historical background.' Here Arlott is expanding on the idea of cricket 'mirroring' society to include regional variations of character. For example, the hard cricket of the northern leagues traditionally reflected the working environment of the English industrial heartland, whereas village cricket in Sussex cr Hampshire is of an altogether different tempo and atmosphere. Similarly, West Indian cricket with its exuberance and flair could only be a product of the sunny way of life in the islands. Arlott has also pointed out that, in common with a select number of other sports, cricket has proved its significance beyond the field of performance by producing art and literature, as well as passing its language into common usage. These themes, in the hands of an Arlott or a Cardus, produce delightful literary essays, but in addition they make a serious contribution to our social history.

What, then, is the historical evidence for this assertion that English cricket has reflected – or, more accurately, been influenced by – the social scene in the country at large? Here one runs into a potential problem – not for a lack of supporting evidence but rather because it can be easy to force-fit the facts in order to prove the point. It is tempting, but surely an oversimplification, to talk of 'Regency Cricket', of 'Victorian' or 'Edwardian' cricket as if each era could be neatly pigeon-holed. In truth, the cricket of these or any other periods was, like the broader social picture itself, too varied to allow hard and fast division. Nevertheless, as the country has evolved gradually from one social and economic style to another, so cricket has been slowly adapted. Perhaps cricket is not a perfect 'mirroring' of society, but certainly it is subject to many of the same driving forces. At this point perhaps we should add one rider to this statement; since the mid-eighteenth century there have always been two distinct types of cricket – the professional or first-class game which attracts paying spectators, and the club, village or schoolboy game played in spare time purely for fun. While the organization and conduct of the former has typically been influenced by outside social forces, the latter has been a more constant and intrinsic part of the nation's everyday life.

To explore further the rationale for this supposed inter-dependence of cricket and society we should look first at the development of the game at least back to the eighteenth and early nineteenth centuries. The cricket of this period has been treated, in sympathy with the prevailing social scene, in the books by Ford and Brookes previously mentioned as well as in other sports histories such as that by H. A. Harris (*Sport in Britain: Its Origins and Development*, Stanley Paul, 1975). They, and others, have traced the way in which the largely folk game of the seventeenth century was developed into the organized professional sport of the Victorian era, largely as a result of outside social influences. Until the mid-1700s cricket, boxing and racing were the only sports that commanded any real attention and, of these, cricket was still regarded as mainly a rural pursuit, principally in the south-east of the country. When, however, one reads in 1801 (J. Strutt, *The Sports and Pastimes of the People of England*) that, 'Cricket of late years is become exceedingly fashionable, being much countenanced by the nobility and gentlemen of fortune,' it is tempting to label this the era of 'Regency Cricket'. While it is true that the world of the bucks and their London and Brighton Society did have an influence on the cricket of the time, it would be foolish to make this generalization. Cricket has never been the sole preserve of just one segment of society, and therein lies one of its most special qualities. Ford is more comprehensive about this period when he writes that cricket held up 'a mirror to the times, to an age of violence, of growing professionalism, of patronage, of foreign travel, of clubs, of jingoism, of drinking and of gambling, and to a society in which, despite the continuing dominance of London, the majority of Englishmen lived still in villages or in small rural towns.' Here, in one sentence, is a clear summary of the way in which the cricket of that period was moulded by the parallel developments in people's everyday lives.

As nineteenth-century Britain was approaching its Industrial Revolution so cricket entered into a revolution of its own. Many of the old characteristics virtually disappeared. Gambling was driven from the game as evidenced by the famous banning of William Lambert (a cricketer as famous then as Botham is today) and the eviction of bookmakers from Lord's in 1818. Patronage by the gentry declined but, above all, the technique of the game was turned upside down by the so-called 'March of Intellect' bowling, or round-arm, which was legalized in 1828. This flavour of modernization and superior intellect in cricket neatly reflected the change in Britain from a largely rural to a more industrialized society. In a more direct way the Industrial Revolution deeply affected cricket, and that was via the introduction of the railway system. This, more than anything else, made William Clarke's touring All-England Eleven possible and thereby helped to evolve the modern form of inter-county, first-class cricket.

If the latter half of the nineteenth century can be broadly described as the age of Victorian expansionism then the parallel in cricket is again clear to see. County clubs sprang up, inter-national tours were instituted and, above all, W. G. Grace expanded the technical dimensions of the game beyond recognition. In the process he achieved a popularity and notoriety previously unheard of for a sportsman. This Victorian expansionism was reflected in other sports too. Whereas in 1860 only cricket and rowing had a code of rules accepted throughout the country, by 1885 athletics, soccer, rugby, tennis, golf, cycling and swimming all had national associations for the purpose. At the same time the philosophy of chivalry and 'playing the game' that has come to be associated with Victorianism left its mark on the cricket of the period, and indeed for much of the twentieth century as well. Mark Girouard in his book *The Return to Camelot: Chivalry and the English Gentleman* (Yale University Press, 1981) has explored the nineteenth-century phenomenon which saw the revival of medieval notions of honour, bravery and self-sacrifice. He shows how this code shaped the character of English society, but it was never better demonstrated than in the field of sport.

Girouard writes:

> Chivalry helped to create the Victorian gentleman; and the Victorian gentleman created, or rather re-created, cricket. Indeed, the whole vast fabric of contemporary sport derives, not just from Victorian England, but from the small percentage of Victorian Englishmen who went to the public schools. The games which public-school men took up or invented, the rules which they laid down for them, the clothes which they wore, the settings and equipment which they devised, the language which they used and the seriousness with which they took the whole business gradually spread down the social scale and out to the rest of the world.

It was this era that really cemented cricket as an integral part of English life and character, that made it the truly 'national game'. As the public schools and universities took to team games as a vehicle for the virtues of fellowship, discipline, leadership and physical fitness, so cricket emerged as the pre-eminent sport. Girouard points out that the moral value of games was given official recognition in 1864 when the Royal Commission on the Public Schools reported that 'the cricket and football fields . . . are not merely places of exercise and amusement: they help to form some of the most valuable social qualities and manly virtues.' *Mens sana in corpore sano* was the motto of the day, and this ethic was perhaps best summed up in Newbolt's famous poem 'Vitai Lampada' with its now-hackneyed invocation to 'Play the game!'

Cricket in late-Victorian England was clearly far removed from the lusty exercise of the previous century when betting and even unscrupulousness were often evident. In this self-cleansing, as so often, the game was simply following in the wake of the society in which it was played. Whether the reverence, almost a sanctity, which became attached to cricket was beneficial has been a matter of debate, but certainly it should not be suggested that the evolution of the 'Gentleman's Game' in any way signalled a decrease in the involvement of other levels of society. The coexistence of a lord and a labourer in the same cricket team has been an ever-present feature since the days when the Duke of Dorset employed and played with Lumpy Stevens.

The one phase in cricket's long history which supports most readily the theory of the game reflecting everyday life is the so-called Golden Age, usually accepted as lasting from around 1895 to 1914. There can be no doubt that there was a certain self-consistency about this period that separates the cricket from all that has occurred before or since. The play and the players were attractive and interesting, and subsequent writers have lent the period a romantic mystique rivalled only by the earlier Hambledon era. Added to this, the Golden Age of cricket falls neatly into the late-Victorian and Edwardian era of British life. David Frith in his book on this subject, makes the connection between cricket and general history:

> They [the players] did, after all, reflect the moods of the life around them. It was a time of complacency, security and opulent pride for Britain and her splendid Empire, and the ascent of wide-girthed 'Teddy' to the throne heralded warm, succulent breezes of gaiety which dislodged and dispersed inhibitions.

To summarize, the over-riding characteristic of both the Edwardian era and the cricket of the day was the existence of 'style'.

C. L. R. James, the West Indian author of one of the finest of cricket books, *Beyond a Boundary*, is another who has taken up the theme of cricket in society; he is particularly perceptive, as one might expect, on the influence of the West Indian way of life, politics and culture on its cricket. This is what he has to say on the Golden Age:

> At any particular period it [the game of cricket] reflects tendencies in the national life . . . In social and political life the Edwardian age was possible only on the solid accumulations of the Victorian era. In cricket it was the same.

In cricketing terms everything seemed changed after the Great War and to some extent this was true of life in general. Patrick Morrah sums up the situation as follows:

> England after 1918 was an exhausted country – physically, morally and financially; rehabilitation was the order of the day. The carefree, self-confident spirit of the Edwardian age was a thing of the past; the new era was grimmer and more earnest, more determined and more utilitarian. Cricket has always reflected the mood of the nation. Edwardian opulence had vanished, and with it opulent batting. The technique of the game was studied more closely than ever, and bowlers set themselves to keep runs

down rather than to take wickets. Economy was the watchword of the day.

The same idea was embraced by Cardus who, writing in 1945, saw the 1920s as a sorry decline from the Golden Age:

> When first-class cricket was played again after the end of the 1914-1918 war, we were given yet another example of what a sensitive plant this cricket is – how quick to respond to atmosphere, how eloquent at any time of the English mood and temper. It was an age of some disillusionment and cynicism; the romantic gesture was distrusted. 'Safety First' was the persistent warning. We saw at once on the cricket field the effect of a dismal philosophy and a debilitated state of national health. Beautiful and brave stroke-play gave way to a sort of trench warfare, conducted behind the sandbag of broad pads. A shrewd professionalism decided on a compromise; enough of pace, pitched just short of a length, and a suggestion of spin and more of swerve, the attack directed on the leg-stump – the main idea being to obtain a reasonably good bowling analysis every season at the expenditure of a minimum of risk and physical endurance. The root cause was the nation's economy. There were now few of the amateur players from the old social mint . . .
>
> An attempt was made by legislators to put an end to negative batting and negative bowling . . . The source of the disease could not be touched by new laws . . . English cricket in the 1920s was, like the country as a whole, psychologically, even spiritually ill; character and skill in cricket were becoming standardised with everything else in the land.

The preceding quote is included at some length partly because it is interesting to imagine the same passage being used to refer to the period after the Second World War. Indeed, when one considers that it is the cricket of Hammond, Bradman, Hobbs, Headley, Larwood, Tate, Gregory, Macdonald, O'Reilly and Grimmett that is being described, it is hard to understand. On the other hand, there was a certain relentlessness that crept into the game at the expense of spontaneity and flair: the remorseless batting of Ponsford and Hutton, the 'win at all costs' captaincy of Armstrong and Jardine. It was this lack of chivalry or adventure – with some notable exceptions – that differentiated the inter-war years from the Golden Age. These years were ones of economic difficulties and high unemployment. Here, the simplistic approach to cricket 'mirroring' society falls down, as the thought of 'Depression Era' cricket is plainly ludicrous. In other ways, though, the desire for restoring the status quo, a resistance to change and a tendency to ignore potential problems were all hallmarks of both society and cricket.

While Cardus was a critic of trends during the inter-war years, some of the most interesting discussions of post-1945 cricket, in terms of social climate, have come from C. L. R. James and the equally respected Yorkshire journalist, J. M. Kilburn. Both have been highly critical, in a saddened rather than vehement manner, about developments in post-war cricket.

James, writing in 1957, having likened Golden Age cricket to the gaiety and style of the Edwardian era, proceeded to compare this with the lacklustre play he was witnessing in England at that time:

> If the glory of the Golden Age is to be found in the specific mental attitudes of the men who made it what it was, the drabness of the prevailing style of play should be sought in the same place. The prevailing attitude of the players of 1890-1914 was daring, adventure, creation. The prevailing attitude of 1957 can be summed up in one word – security . . . The cricketers of today play the cricket of a specialised stratum, that of functionaries in the welfare state.

Here, James is not so much linking cricket with the social surroundings but more specifically pointing the finger at the individual players themselves. His point regarding the security-conscious mental state brought on by the welfare state should be given some respect especially since it comes from a Marxist with a strong feeling for social issues. We can assume, therefore, that he was, in principle, a supporter of the welfare programmes of the post-war years, yet he still recognized that what is good for the individual may not be good for the welfare of cricket. While this argument of 'welfare state cricket' is superficially attractive to describe safety-first tactics and the growing tendency towards cricket matches as wars of attrition, there are problems with it. Firstly, the whole question of the 'attitude' of an individual or group of individuals is far too complicated and varied to be pigeon-holed as 'welfare state mind'. Secondly, as we have seen, while the scoring-rates of Bradman, Hammond and company may have been high before the war, the tendency towards avoiding defeat at all costs had crept in long before the welfare state. No, this was a gradual process and while the evolution of a security consciousness in post-war Britain may have encouraged the development of unadventurous cricket, the blame cannot be laid squarely on the players' attitudes. There were also parallels in other sports. In soccer, the centre-half dropped back to become a last line of defence, and later was joined by the 'double centre-half' and the 'sweeper'. Rugby Union was beset by dull strategic battles dominated by kicking for touch rather than an open passing game. The post-war disease was contagious and in some sports has never really been arrested.

Whatever the reasons, though, there seems to be general agreement that, after the initial post-war fling of the late forties, the game of cricket in Britain went through a steady decline as a public entertainment. Not necessarily a decline in playing skill (although some would argue this also) but certainly a less desirable entertainment to watch and, for some, a less alluring game to play (here we are talking purely at the first-class level; the club and village game remained largely immune). This continued at least into the sixties and, some would argue, continues today. Even the most traditional diehard, however, must admit that the development through the late sixties and seventies of one-day cricket, of Sunday play, sponsorship, overseas stars and all the other paraphernalia of the modern game, has brought about a revolution in cricket and has increased public interest. The new style may not please everyone but that has always been the case, dating back to the protracted arguments regarding first round-arm and later over-arm bowling. Why, even W. G. Grace was criticized for playing 'boundary' rather than 'real' cricket.

Anyway, the main theme of this book will be that the foundations for the modern game were laid in what can be viewed as a well-defined cricketing era roughly bounded by the years 1946-63. The 'revolution' may have occurred since then but the driving forces were all put into place during those years, a period which, for many, constituted cricket's low point. J. M. Kilburn certainly has written to this effect stating that the 'trickle of trends that began in the 1950s swelled to flood-waters through the 1960s.' He supports the view that cricket has indeed undergone a revolution and that recent developments constitute the first serious change in the game since the time of W. G. Grace:

Cricketers of 1900 would have looked slightly old-fashioned

in the cricket of 1950 but they would not have appeared altogether out of their element; in 1970 they would have been bewildered in an unimagined world. There was no precise moment of beginning for the revolution, no single cause to be isolated and defined. Cricket is the people who play and govern it. They, or their outlook, changed and their change was influenced by the circumstances of contemporary life. Cricket thinking reflected the social and economic thinking of the times and from the new morality of society created a new morality for itself.

Its [the revolution of the sixties] accomplishment had been more rapid and more fundamental than the most rabid of cricket anarchists or iconoclasts had contemplated. The gates of tradition were found to have surprisingly flimsy locks and hinges.

So, what precisely was the social background during this unmistakable slipping of cricket from its traditional pedestal as the 'National Game'? For much of the period, certainly right through the fifties, the country was dominated by the after-effects of the war, not only in economics but also in terms of attitude and behaviour. It was a period characterized by marked (some would say radical or revolutionary) changes in the fabric of everyday life, many of which, we will see, had an effect on cricket. These changes can be broadly grouped under the two classifications of an increased cultural permissiveness or freedom, and the tremendous impact made by scientific or technological advances. Both of these trends were instrumental in the evolution of the early post-war austerity/recovery phase into the so-called 'affluent society' of the late fifties, the era of Macmillan's catch phrase 'You've never had it so good!' We now know that this period of comparative affluence flattered to deceive in some respects, but even in today's somewhat depressed economic climate, after the ravages of inflation, the average level of prosperity and material comfort in Britain is a marked improvement on pre-war days. Certainly, the influence of true poverty has been all but eliminated.

What were the specifics to support this assertion of a period of dramatic change? The umbrella of cultural permissiveness is not intended to suggest sexual freedoms, although that was a small part of it, but embraces the loosening of a wide variety of controls on British society. These include such diverse examples as the reduced voting age, the legalization of gambling, availability of abortion, the Women's Liberation movement (dating from war-time work for women), and the introduction of commercial television. To this more progressive environment was added the gradual removal of temporary post-war rationing and, ultimately, the development of the modern 'consumer' society. The reduction in censorship, increase in crime and juvenile delinquency and a gradual increase in vandalism and drug offences all contributed to a massive upheaval of the traditional values of society. Fashions also reflected this upheaval and were changing as fast as every other facet of life: the wasp-waisted New Look, the bikini, the teddy boy and the mini-skirt came and went in rapid succession.

In education there were far greater numbers staying at school to the age of eighteen and subsequently going to university. This, and the increased demand for teachers that it brought, certainly affected the recruitment of cricketers. The developing welfare state was manifest in the introduction of the Health Service, family allowances, unemployment benefit and legal aid for the poor. Everywhere you looked changes were happening at a furious rate.

The impact of technology was massive – much of it, like the development of the jet engine and synthetic fabrics, hastened by the war. Scientific methods revolutionized farming, decimated the cotton industry (via synthetics) and radically improved medicine. Industry changed as society progressed; there were more service jobs (banking, insurance, communications, enter-tainment, etc.) than traditional manufacturing or farming work. For this reason there may have been less incentive to escape manual labour for a sporting career. Television quickly grew to dominate in the fifties. Motor cars thrived after the end of petrol rationing in 1950 and had an enormous impact on travel, holidays, town planning and industry. Indeed, leisure itself became an industry as the number of people with two weeks paid holiday rose from three million in 1948 to twelve and a quarter million in 1956. In company with this, people began to take up participative sports like golf, sailing, climbing, camping, fishing, tennis, tenpin bowling and even bingo. Organized team sports declined in popularity as a result.

What has all this social history to do with a book on cricket? The answer must be a great deal, if we are to understand the enormous changes that occurred in cricket at the very same time as everyday life was also changing so radically. To quote Arlott yet again, 'Games are as truly part of the history of a nation as its work, wars and art. They are a reflection of the social life of the people, changing with it and conditioned by its changes in economy, religion and politics.' In particular, we will see that the increased permissiveness of the fifties and sixties, the loosening of traditional codes of behaviour, was most certainly reflected in cricket and other sports. The chapters which follow trace the increase of professionalism in cricket, the subsequent domination of monetary considerations and the inevitable decline in conduct and behaviour standards of some of the leading players. While this has occurred there has been a steady decline in the general level of spectator interest, largely obscured by increased media attention on 'big' events and the star players. Test matches and tours have multiplied alarmingly at the expense of the grassroots of the game.

The dependence of this on the larger changes in society is proved by the almost identical scenarios that have been followed by other sports. Arthur Marwick, in his study *British Society Since 1945*, observed this link between social evolution and soccer:

> In so many ways, then, British society seemed to have broken out of the straitjacket of dullness and conformity which had pinioned it since Victorian times . . . there was a new hedonism abroad in the land; life was lived with greater gusto than ever it had been since the evangelicals set their stamp upon the mores of the middle class. A symbolic case study was provided by Association Football. The abolition in 1962 of the maximum wage . . . enabled the best players to escape into a world of high earnings which, though most players remained working-class in background and manner, had something of that veneer of classlessness to be found in other branches of the entertainments industry. Football became fashionable.

Much the same could be said of cricket since the Packer revolution put more money into the players' pockets. There is, however, a negative side to these inflated salaries. Once Jimmy Hill had been successful in abolishing the maximum wage for footballers, in 1962, the game saw a steady decline in ethics and behaviour. High wages are accompanied by inflated transfer fees, bribery is a recurring menace and the young star players are often ill-equipped to handle their situation. The hooligan element among spectators only serves to exacerbate the situation. Tennis has also seen many of the afflictions that have occurred in post-war cricket. From a situation in which the best players in the world were part of a Packer-style professional circus and the amateurs were really shamateurs, the sport became 'open' around 1968. Since then, money has come to dominate and the old-guard traditionalists who remember tennis as a gentleman's game are appalled by the antics of McEnroe and Nastase. Rugby Union could clearly develop along similar lines as the game becomes more professional in approach, and athletics may not be far behind, although golf, where huge sums of money are at stake, has largely avoided this problem.

This is the negative side of permissiveness in sport. Cricket, however, also benefited in some ways from this trend since it was a loosening of conventional chains that resulted in the one-day games, Sunday play and overseas stars in county cricket. While they have become a mixed blessing, their value in resurrecting the game should not be underestimated.

Throughout this book we will study in greater detail the effects that social developments had on post-war cricket – from the rise of television to compulsory National Service; from the consumer society to the rate of immigration. The following chapters will trace their impact on cricket and, in passing, on other sports. While the prose will not fit the romantic code of a Cardus, hopefully it will not fall into the dry language of pure social history. We should not lose sight of the fact that, rather than merely a topic for detailed analysis, cricket is above all a game watched, played and enjoyed by people. At times it can achieve high drama, at others it can inspire art and literature. At the highest level it may be a business operation, but basically it is a simple part of everyday life.

2
The Early Post-War Cricket Scene

The chapters which follow will give a detailed account of the important changes in English cricket during the post-war years. Financial issues, the amateur question, controversies, one-day cricket, overseas stars, Packer – these will all be discussed in the light of cricket's past history, its subsequent development and the everyday social environment. Before embarking on this analysis, however, it seems appropriate to broadly set the cricketing scene. While recent events seem crystal clear, post-war cricket is now forty years old and the 1940s and 1950s, at least, can be looked at with a hopefully dispassionate historical perspective. While not describing each season in detail, a flavour of the period can be captured and some of the important trends highlighted.

Although there was no first-class cricket played in Britain during 1940-44, the game did not completely disappear during those five summers. There were a number of high-quality scratch elevens, overseas forces teams, some one-day county games, and much club cricket. It was not until the surrender of Germany in May 1945, however, that any seriously organized matches with first-class status were played. It was only a couple of weeks after VE day when 70,000 people poured into Lord's over the Whitsun weekend to see the first of the summer's so-called 'Victory Tests' between England and a strong team of Australian servicemen. For the thousands, many in uniform, some in their new 'demob' suits, who queued to pay a shilling at the turnstiles it was almost a symbolic celebration of the end of the war. The cricket was exuberant and exciting, as one might expect with Hutton, Hammond, Ames, Hassett and Miller celebrating along with the spectators.

On 5 July that year two events occurred that were significant in their own worlds. While Britons went to the polls for the first time in a decade, Kennington Oval was officially returned to the charge of the Surrey club. The result of the former was the election of Attlee's Labour government to succeed the wartime coalition. Peacetime called for social change, revolution some were to say, and the socialists claimed the right to implement the ideas of the hoped-for 'New Age'. The return of The Oval, however, was cricket's example of how the after-effects of war were felt in those early months of peace. Over four million houses, plus numerous offices and factories, had been destroyed or damaged in the bombing, but mercifully the historic pavilions at the two major London grounds escaped unharmed. Recovery from this destruction was complicated by the fact that, although victorious in war, the nation's economy was in ruins.

The Oval was in the heart of London's devastation and had been hit by high explosives and countless incendiaries during the blitz. Bert Lock, a former Surrey cricketer, was appointed groundsman upon his demobilization in October 1945 and this is how he described what he found:

> The square had not been touched for six years, and was covered with long, coarse grass full of weeds. The outfield had been used for a searchlight, gun-site and a prisoner-of-war camp, with miles of barbed wire supported by 1000 poles all in concrete two feet deep. There were four huts erected on one-foot-thick concrete bases, with a number of drains in between. At the Vauxhall end were large pits. Weeds grown to a great height covered the whole area (I even found a bramble bush). There was also an 'assault course' at the Vauxhall end which had to be removed, and thousands of bricks from the bomb-blasted West wall. Fencing and stands were in a shocking state of repair, and hundreds of seats calling for a new coat of paint. In all 11,000 square yards of ground were levelled and over 35,000 turfs laid. I obtained these from close to Gravesend, where I walked for miles over the marshes to find this almost weed-free turf.

Despite these enormous difficulties, the nets were up and play began again in April 1946, the first full season of county cricket after the war.

In contrast, Lord's was kept active for cricket throughout the war, despite requisitioning of the pavilion by the RAF, and many thrilling one-day matches of a high standard were played before large crowds. In some ways it is surprising that these games did not suggest the adoption of one-day cricket competitions when the war was over, but this was to be delayed for a further eighteen years. Large crowds watched most of the wartime matches at Lord's but the Victory Tests broke all records. The total attendance at headquarters for the summer of 1945 was not far short of a million, a staggering figure that compares with many subsequent full seasons of county and Test cricket.

The unofficial Test Matches of 1945 were highlights of a summer which witnessed a succession of major events. Two weeks after the general election, the first atom bomb fell on Japan and precipitated total surrender on 14 August. On that same day it seemed to many that Australian cricket had also surrendered when Reuters reported: 'It is confirmed that Bradman is very unlikely ever to play in big cricket again.' Needless to say, the premature nature of this statement was to be forcibly demonstrated over the next three years.

The mood of the British public during the five years of Attlee's government has been described by some as one of jubilation and excitement at the challenge ahead, and by others as a continual round of grey drabness caused by post-war economic and material shortages. As always, the truth is probably somewhere in between. Major John Freeman, in his reply to the King's Speech on the opening of the new Parliament, captured the feelings of many:

> The country is conscious of the seriousness of the years that lie ahead; but our people are not depressed by the outlook . . . on the contrary, on every side is a spirit of high adventure, of gay determination, a readiness to experiment, to take reasonable risks, to stake high in this magnificent venture of rebuilding our civilization.

In cricketing terms, that mood was reflected in the carefree play of the first few summers of peacetime. Crowds filled the county grounds as never before, batsmen dominated the bowlers, and national heroes such as Hammond, Compton and Edrich displayed that 'spirit of high adventure'. In one aspect, however, the cricket establishment disapproved of the new spirit of daring shown in the first season of the resumed county championship. A number of rain-ruined matches, notably one between Somerset and Glamorgan, were resolved by the captains agreeing on so-called 'freak' first innings declarations to enable a result. Such declarations had occurred in a small way before, in 1931, and had been strongly discouraged by MCC. This time the chairman of the newly formed Society of Cricket Statisticians (later the Cricket Society), Anthony Weigell, wrote to *The Times* to protest the 'travesty of a first class game', and requested that the Somerset/ Glamorgan match be 'struck out of the records'. A follow-up letter asserted that 'County cricket, and, of course, international cricket, is not played primarily to attract the public to the matches.' A further correspondent thankfully pointed out to readers that this was 'arrant nonsense', but MCC sided with the traditionalists. In an announcement which recalled the similar warning of 1931 they stated, 'It is clear that the laws of cricket do not provide for collaboration of this kind.' Later it was announced that umpires would report any suspected collusion and that MCC would deduct championship points if necessary. This reaction, like that of 1931, is in sharp contrast with the prevailing attitude in later years where 'sporting' declarations to overcome lost time and/or slow play have been openly encouraged in the name of 'brighter' cricket. In fact, this is just one of the many areas in which cricket administrators had to perform a sharp about-face and upset the traditionalists when faced with the disastrous, and possibly fatal, financial position of county cricket in the early sixties.

This spirit of adventure and abandon on the cricket field reflected, as we have noted, the mood of the people even if it was in vivid contrast to the low material quality of life in the forties. The decline in cricket's popularity which was to characterize the fifties and sixties was never suspected in the palmy days of those first few post-war summers. The high attendances of 1945 continued and cricket's finances were as healthy as they had been in the entire history of the game. Free of the cares of war and without the many alternative leisure pursuits of later years, people flocked to see the farewells of the pre-war giants like Hammond and Bradman, and the precious few years that remained for the pre-war youngsters – Hutton, Compton, Edrich – so cruelly robbed of their cricketing prime. There were deprivations and make-shift arrangements in the first full season of 1946 but nobody seemed to mind. Surrey, in common with most counties, had to appeal for extra clothing coupons from their supporters just so that the team could be properly kitted out; N. H. Bennett, the new county captain, wore the club blazer of R. deW. K. Winlaw after it was returned to The Oval by his relatives following Winlaw's death in a flying accident. In the Varsity match the players also wore borrowed blazers but no amount of inconvenience could dampen people's enthusiasm.

The summer of 1947, the second year after the resumption of

normal Test and county cricket, has gone down as one of the most
memorable seasons in the entire history of the game. John Arlott,
then just beginning to build his unique reputation, has perfectly
captured the feelings of those who lived through that season:

> For me it was a summer of joys which, it had sometimes
> seemed during the war years, could never return. There was a
> warmth of feeling and an enthusiasm abroad which has never
> since been recaptured in any English cricket season.

The brilliance of the cricket that year appeared in sharp relief
against the backdrop of a largely drab lifestyle for the majority of
people. Widespread rationing continued and, although certificates
for cricket equipment were no longer required, there were serious
shortages for the club player. This was the year of the man-power
crisis and British Double Summer Time. Some county matches
were played from one until eight o'clock, with no lunch interval,
to enable spectators to work a full day before going to the ground.
Before the season began there had been a very real threat of the
Government banning all mid-week sport but the Home Secretary,
Chuter Ede, himself a very keen cricket spectator, ruled that
attendances were too low to significantly affect production or
power usage.

In some ways, however, the strikingly attractive cricket being
played and watched by so many was just one example of the
attempts being made to compensate for the shortages. Even the
lucky ones might only be housed in 'prefabs' sparsely filled with
'utility' furniture, but the cinemas and theatres, as well as the
cricket grounds, have never been so full. People were prepared to
put up with endless queues, late trains, and boarded-up shop
windows, for a year or two at least. Cigarettes may have been in
short supply but the entertainment available was to be enjoyed as
never before. It was in this year of 1947 that Dior launched his
famous 'New Look' in female fashions. The swirling, mid-calf
skirts and wasp-waists were a perfectly natural reaction to wartime
overalls and uniforms, and they became a familiar sight almost
overnight.

We need not describe the cricket details of that season since
they have been recounted with accuracy and feeling in an entire
book by John Arlott (*Vintage Summer: 1947*, Eyre & Spottiswoode, 1967). Suffice it to say, the joyous cricket of 1947 was a
not insignificant part of the post-war recovery for many people.
The apparently trivial fact that one could open the morning

paper and read cricket scores after six blank years was a source of great pleasure to countless thousands. The other side of the coin, however, the hardship and sacrifice – the 'lean years of peace' – should not be forgotten. Following the brilliant weather of the 1947 summer, the winter was one of the worst ever, and brought the words 'austerity' and 'shortage' into sharp focus. While the MCC tourists basked in the West Indian heat, persistent electricity cuts at home meant that English families ate a cold breakfast by candlelight, walked through unlit streets, up motionless escalators before huddling in their overcoats at the office desk. The BBC suspended broadcasts and the spirit of the blitz was needed yet again. This gloom could, indeed, have spread to cricket fields in 1948 if the Duke of Wellington had had his way. Regarding the need for more farm land, he announced, 'There is cricket for instance; it takes the maximum space and the maximum time, while providing the minimum amount of exercise, and I am not sure whether a bankrupt country should indulge in it.'

At this time food, clothing, petrol, coal and other necessities were still rationed and shortages continued until the early fifties. In company with this, English cricket soon began to show its own signs of austerity on the field of play, despite the successful 1947 season, the exciting play and the huge attendances. Australia had chalked up eleven victories during the series of 1946/7, 1948 and 1950/1 before England could manage their first post-war win against the old enemy. Crushing defeats were also suffered at the hands of the West Indies in 1947/8 and 1950, and during one disastrous period seven successive Tests were lost outright. Hutton, Washbrook, Compton and Edrich provided a solid enough batting line-up, but the bowling was pitifully thin with Bedser and Wright often very expensive wicket-takers. This lack of Test match success simply reflected the low standard of the county championship. Many of the older pre-war players, many well over forty, gallantly turned out for their counties although they could not seriously expect to recapture their former skills. Many of the younger replacements showed initial form which only flattered to deceive. Above all, there was a sharp decline in the availability of good amateurs.

Cricket was not the only sport to suffer in this way. In 1948, the year that Bradman's Australians ruthlessly exposed these inherent cricket problems, English sporting reputations were at an all-time low. The Olympics were held in London with America winning thirty-eight events to Britain's three. Wimbledon was dominated by 'Georgeous Gussie' Moran, our two world boxing titles were lost and the soccer team experienced a succession of defeats. The gallant British amateur spirit could no longer compete in the modern world of international sport. By 1948 MCC was proposing a delay in the planned programme of tours because the standard of English cricket was taking so long to recover from the war. A resolution was passed which prohibited a tour to England in the season following an Australian visit, and although this idea was abandoned, the next home Ashes series was postponed from 1952 to 1953. By 1950, there were increasing calls for the restructuring of domestic cricket as many recognized that despite the high public interest there were serious problems. In fact, by the close of this initial post-war period we begin to see with increasing regularity the comments and discussions so common to the cricket scene over the next twenty years. After the 1951 season Colonel Rait Kerr, the Secretary of MCC, announced that attendances for the year had sharply decreased, and in his view this was linked to the increased percentage of drawn games – 50% as opposed to only 25% in 1938, 1939, 1946 and 1947. Although partly offset by increased membership, this apparent decline was felt to be caused by increased defensive tactics – leg-side bowling and field setting – and the increase of professionalism.

Another familiar topic of discussion in 1951 was the need to stem the flow of overseas players into county cricket. Can it really be thirty-four years ago that the Advisory County Cricket Committee was saying: 'While these cricketers in small numbers play a useful part in county cricket, a large increase in their number would prevent the development of English players'? At least nobody can say we had no warning.

The more one studies the cricket of the past, the more it becomes apparent that the troubles and problems of today's game have nearly all been seen or forecast before. In 1950 there were misunderstandings regarding fast bowlers leaving the field for a rub-down and returning to bowl in the same session. In that same year a member of the Warwickshire ground staff, aggrieved at his dismissal by the club, spread weed-killer on the square and put sawdust in the engine of the mower. Even cricket's 'holy of holies' – the Long Room at Lord's – did not escape. Surely it could not have been a member of the club who stole the 1787 Golden Guinea (the year in which MCC was founded) from its glass case in that same year of 1950? As long ago as 1948 umpires were warned to look out for bowlers using resin, oil or grease to preserve the shine on the ball; the more recent allegations are nothing new. At that time, however, there was even a feeling that the use of good old-fashioned spit or honest sweat to polish the ball should be discouraged. Doug Wright, who habitually licked his fingers before bowling, was reprimanded by an umpire on the MCC tour to South Africa in 1948/9, and the following lines appeared in *The Times*.

> As finger-bowls would be denied
> To cricketers (fastidious souls),
> So Wright claims right upon his side
> And having licked his fingers, bowls.

The season of 1953 was another which proved a landmark in the post-war history of cricket and, indeed, in the life of the nation. The year was dominated, of course, by the coronation of Queen Elizabeth, but of the many other notable events England's regaining the Ashes after nineteen long years was certainly a highlight. In a Test series of swaying fortunes Hutton's team just stayed ahead thanks to the magnificent bowling of Alec Bedser, the famous rearguard action of Watson and Bailey, the spin of Laker and Lock – in fact, a very strong England team had finally come together after the humiliation of the immediate post-war years. Its strength lay in its depth and in a blend of talented youth and some truly great old campaigners. The emotional scenes at The Oval after Compton and Edrich steered the side to the clinching victory have gone down in English folklore. Brian Johnston's television commentary and shout of 'England have won the Ashes!' will be replayed as long as cricket exists.

Hutton and Compton were not the only sporting heroes to gladden the heart that year. Gordon Richards, already a legend in the world of horse-racing and the greatest favourite of the punters, won his first Derby at the age of forty-nine, riding Pinza. (Incidentally, watched by Lindwall and Miller, who missed the Australian match for the occasion.) Richards was knighted that year as was Jack Hobbs, about whom an unkind word has surely never been written, uttered or thought – excepting, of course, by a few perspiring bowlers. The tremendous bond between the British public and their best-loved sportsmen – like Hobbs, Compton and Richards – is yet another example of the inter-relationship between professional sport and everyday life.

Another who shared this empathy was Stanley Matthews. 1953 was the legendary year in which he brought Blackpool from the brink of defeat to a 4-3 victory over Bolton Wanderers in the Cup Final. This was the time when footballers wore baggy shorts and earned less than £15 per week to which was added a £10 bonus for the victorious Blackpool players. This year also saw a new record transfer fee when the astronomical sum of £30,000 was lavished on Trevor Ford. Homely and nostalgic though this image of football seems, 1953 also brought the most famous defeat ever suffered by England's national team – the 6-3 drubbing by Hungary, the first ever loss on home soil. Mostly, though, it was a glorious year for the home-grown sportsman. Everest was conquered and even in defeat there were English heroes in the narrowest of losses in the Ryder Cup.

The visiting Australians who had toured in 1948 noticed the progress being made from austerity to affluence. Jack Fingleton wrote, 'London has improved out of all knowledge . . . There is a vibrant note on all sides. In 1948 the city was low spirited, people were poorly dressed and the food was in keeping. Now London is brightly painted.' Part of the enthusiasm and colour was, of course, due to the Coronation, but even in a wet summer the great sporting events also seemed to rise to the occasion.

Despite this fervour and excitement surrounding the Ashes, however, one could not escape from the fact that much of the county cricket was being played at a low standard, on poor pitches and at a slower tempo. Neville Cardus, admittedly a man filled with nostalgia for the Golden Age, was moved to write to *The Times* in a most desolate fashion. Referring to a newspaper report of Matthews' Cup Final in which football was called the 'Game of the People', he found he could no longer claim that title for cricket. On Cup Final day he had been at Lord's: 'I felt pretty certain I had been attending a decaying contemporary industry which, but for the artificial respiration applied from time to time by the Australians, would before long pass into the hands of the brokers and gradually disappear, not greatly lamented, into profound oblivion.' As always, C. B. Fry, even at the age of eighty-one, could be relied on for a hearty reply in which he commented, 'Even if it ceases to be played or to be watched, may not a game remain national in the sense of being most consonant with the character and ideals of a people?'

This was really the beginning of the era when England's successful Test match performances helped to disguise these alleged deficiencies in the county game and, indeed, in the entertainment value and quality of the Tests themselves. While we will discuss the influence of outside social forces as reasons for cricket's apparent decline in popularity – alternative leisure, cynical attitudes, etc. – much of the blame for the style of play in the fifties and sixties must be laid at the sub-standard pitches generally being produced in England. These resulted in an over-haul of batting techniques, virtual disappearance of certain types of bowler, introduction of new laws and conditions and, some would add, a reduction in playing standard.

On studying the history of this period, however, one finds that motives for these changes were entirely honourable. As the forties came to a close there was a growing feeling among many in cricket that the balance between bat and ball had tipped too far in favour of the batsman. This had certainly been the case before the war when massive run-scoring was often prevalent, and in England the interruption of the war years harmed the bowlers (particularly fast ones) far more than the batsmen. Compton, Edrich, Hutton, Hardstaff and the rest were largely plundering some very aged and sub-standard county bowling attacks. Immediately after the war, Nobby Clark, Reg Perks and Alf Gover were probably the fastest in the country, although they were very much past their pre-war best. In retrospect it seems strange to try to legislate against the Bradmans, Hammonds and Comptons but that is precisely what was proposed. As early as 1947 Douglas Jardine suggested the use of a smaller ball in order to facilitate spin. When a larger seam was introduced the following year, Jardine claimed that this would help seamers and swingers whereas his idea would only aid spin. 'An ounce of spin and length would prove a better prescription than a pound of pace and swerve.' This from Jardine, the father of bodyline!

By 1952 it was decided that the same idea should be officially investigated by MCC, and an elaborate series of trials was instigated. Throughout 1953 the new smaller and lighter balls were tested by some of the country's leading cricketers and coaches who unanimously pronounced them an improvement for swing, seam and spin bowlers. Even Ray Lindwall took time out from the Australians' tour to try the ball. He concluded that if it were introduced he would be prepared to continue his illustrious career for at least another ten years! Throughout 1955, though, when the new ball was used in a series of non-county first-class matches, it was strangely found by most players to provide no significant advantage, and some even preferred the larger ball. Since by now the pendulum had already swung in favour of the bowler, the idea was finally abandoned altogether and has not been resurrected.

The bowler's rise to supremacy had in fact been achieved by a far more unsatisfactory development – the counties began to prepare pitches poor enough to guarantee a result. The danger in tampering with wickets in this way is that as well as reducing the dominance of the batsman, one also changes the whole style of cricket that can be played. The run-scoring that is possible cannot be made in an attractive way.

Wilfred Wooller, writing in 1952, had proposed the following highly original theory: 'To my way of thinking, the Groundsmen should be instructed to prepare wickets which suit their own particular type of bowlers.' The rationale for this was that bowlers' wickets produce interesting cricket and inevitably fewer drawn matches. Wooller cited the tremendous interest and huge crowds enjoyed by Lancashire in 1950 when the Old Trafford wicket was tailor-made for the spinners Hilton, Tattersall and Berry. Similarly, Gloucestershire supporters were happy when the Bristol wicket was perfect for Tom Goddard in 1947. The following years were to see some very sporting wickets at The Oval and again the home crowd were happy. By contrast, the batting paradise at Trent Bridge was a soul-destroying experience for bowlers and inevitable drawn matches certainly did not attract the spectators.

The story of the Bristol wicket is an interesting one. Between the wars it was a perfect batting strip, the high clay content resulting in the legendary 'billiard table' surface. In 1946, it was proposed that the following season's Test Trial game be played there but the idea was squashed because of the one-sided playing surface. On professional advice the county added sand to balance the clay and the resulting pitches were summed up by the Somerset captain, Jack Meyer, as 'like batting on Weston-super-Mare beach'. Before the 1950 season Lancashire announced that the heavy roller would be withdrawn from use at Old Trafford and watering would be restricted in order to restore a balance between bat and ball. Like Gloucestershire they clearly over-compensated and had to redress the balance somewhat in 1951, but success certainly came their way and the championship title was shared. Similarly, the Edgbaston wicket of 1953 was notorious for the presence of small pebbles in the topsoil – one player even found the handle of a cup and a rusty nail.

Throughout the early fifties the spin bowlers had a field-day. Many of the more successful counties fielded as many as three spinners in their sides. Surrey had Laker, Lock and Eric Bedser, Lancashire's trio have been mentioned and Gloucester could choose from Cook, Wells, Mortimore and, later, Allen. In 1950 the first-class averages showed only one non-spinner in the first ten places. As well as those already mentioned, Wardle, Walsh, Hollies and Wright were perhaps the leading exponents. The spinners' reign was to be shortlived, however, for within a single cricketing generation they became almost extinct, again through meddling with the wickets. When it was eventually realized that these underprepared pitches were breaking up too early the quickest remedy for the groundsmen was to leave more grass on the wicket. Fast bowlers learned to slow down, pitch shorter, polish the ball (even raise the seam) and rewards duly came their way. This trend increased as the late fifties turned into the sixties. Colin Cowdrey has even said that England at home would probably have been more successful with an attack comprised of Shackleton, Jackson and Cartwright rather than the likes of Trueman and Statham.

E. W. Swanton has described the dramatic change that underwent The Oval wicket after this move to force more 'sporting' pitches.

An Oval spectator of the thirties who returned after 20 years' absence would have rubbed his eyes bewildered. Gone was the fast outfield – in its place a lush green, wonderfully smooth cushion. Gone was the superb batting wicket. The idiosyncrasies of the pitch now were a springy bounce, a disposition to allow the ball to move freely off the seam on the first day and to take an increasing amount of spin.

Doug Insole, who played there often enough, had a different perspective on The Oval wickets of the fifties:

I have a feeling that The Oval came very near to supplying the right sort of pitch, but that Lock and Laker spoiled it for everybody. These two were so far ahead of anybody else in English cricket – or world cricket for that matter – that the slightest encouragement from the pitch made them almost unplayable, while lesser mortals had difficulty in turning the ball at all.

The Oval and other wickets around the country did begin to show some improvement around the end of the fifties due to the introduction of full covering of pitches before, during and after games. This did not stop the production of green wickets, however, and by 1962 the pattern of bowling had come full circle. Bill Bowes was able to write, 'Seam bowlers are the basis of any hopes entertained by any county of winning the championship . . . The finger spin bowler is not really needed by any county attack of today.' The following year the ACCC took another move in the continual see-saw between legislation and ingenuity by strongly requesting less grass be left on wickets. In fact, the counties were within one vote of banning the polishing of the ball – a step that was experimentally taken in 1967.

The prevailing wickets, as we have noted, had an over-whelming effect on the style of play being offered in county cricket. At the same time, partly due to the new LBW law in effect since 1937, batting gradually moved from an off-side bias to a largely leg-side game. J. M. Kilburn, again in his role as critic of a younger generation, had no doubt that this was symptomatic of a post-war trend towards indulgence and cynicism:

> From 1946 onwards bowlers, in keeping with the character of their times, began to concentrate on the easier ways of earning their money. The age of the inswinger followed. Batting was cribbed, cabined and confined by the so-called negative attack of bowling, at all paces, directed towards the leg-side and supported by constraining field-settings.

The batsmen of the day argued that even the legendary names of the past would have been powerless to produce flowing cover-drives against inswing bowling aimed at the leg stump. Doug Insole has claimed that the cricket of this era was of a higher standard than before the war for the simple reason that it was so difficult to score runs attractively:

> Far be it from me to suggest to my elders and betters that tactical advances had brought about an improvement in the game as a spectacle. In fact, I am perfectly willing to concede that, for the uninitiated spectator, it was probably much more fun in the not-so-distant past. But I am absolutely convinced that the game as played today is not a scrap less skilful than it was and that, for the batsman at least, it is much more difficult.

This subject provides a perfect example of the difference in outlook so often found between those who play professional cricket and those who watch and write about it. Kilburn could almost have been answering Insole's viewpoint when he wrote:

> Gradually the players became prisoners of their own sophistication. They undertook a technical exercise, expert in execution, satisfying to participants, maybe, but unrelated to concerns of the wider world.

While blame for the development of restrictive bowling and slow scoring can be partly laid at the door of the groundsman and the legislator, there is one aspect of modern cricket – perhaps the most insidious – which is purely a function of the players' attitude, namely slow over-rates. For too many years now this seems to have been a universal problem, solved only by legislation and fines. It was in the fifties, however, that the habit first began to appear. After the England tour of the West Indies in 1953/4, during which the practice brought some harsh comment, the counties were first asked to keep records of their over-rates. Some blamed Len Hutton for starting the trend, but he was simply an early user of a tactic whose time had arrived. E. W. Swanton has written as follows:

> It would be dishonest to conclude that Len Hutton's influence on English cricket was unreservedly admirable. Apart from his attitude to the opposition . . . he must have either originated or connived at the slowing-down of the over-rate as a tactical ploy. I blush now to recall the prolonged booing of the New Year's Day crowd of 65,000 at Melbourne as England spent the whole five hours getting through 54 overs.

Matters were made a lot worse by the simultaneous emergence of slow over-rates and defensive leg-theory. Although Warwick Armstrong had used similar tactics in 1921 it was during the fifties that instances became commonplace. Alex Bannister pointed out the damage such questionable tactics could do when he wrote, 'My view is that leg-theory is the most polished and advanced plan yet devised by the misplaced genius of man to empty cricket grounds.'

Turning now to more positive developments in these early post-war years we have mentioned that this was an era characterized by dramatic strides in science and technology. While cricket was largely untouched by this, it did benefit to some extent in the areas of travel and communications. Travel by aeroplane is such an accepted feature today, and so essential for the inflated number of international tours, that it is taken for granted. It is hard to believe that as recently as 1962 the MCC touring side arrived in Australia by ship (admittedly having flown as far as Aden). Before the war there had been isolated examples of cricket teams flying – E. W. Swanton's Arabs to Jersey in 1935 and H. M. Martineau's XI to Egypt in 1939. In 1946, however, the Indians became the first touring team to arrive in England by air, in small separate groups in case of disaster. They were also innovative enough to travel from Cardiff to Portsmouth by Dakota, thereby cutting the travel time from five hours by train to just forty minutes by air. That winter MCC flew from Adelaide to Melbourne but only because of a rail strike, and it was not until the 1953/4 tour to the West Indies that the traditional long ocean voyage was dispensed with.

In the area of communications a small improvement was made in catering to the public when loudspeakers were installed at Lord's for the 1948 season. This apparently helpful innovation was greeted by *The Times* in hysterical fashion: 'Lord's has been invaded by mechanical monsters properly at home in the gaunt stands of football grounds.' In a sharp about-face, however, the same newspaper criticized the Warwickshire committee for requesting spectators not to play radios at the ground. This was 'playing Canute against the tides of progress', and it was forecast that individuals would soon have their own personal television on hand while watching a match. Although this has taken a long time to occur it is now a common sight at American football and baseball games. By 1950 televised cricket was still something of a novelty although rapid strides were being made. When the third Test at Trent Bridge was televised it was the most northerly outside broadcast yet attempted by the BBC. A major talking point at this time was whether the commentators should use the players' Christian names or not. P. F. Warner was one who objected to this, and *The Times* argued, 'What mere name can rival the impressiveness of C. B. Fry, L. C. H. Palairet, J. T. Tyldesley or J. T. Hearne?'

Another improvement in communications was the inauguration of the telephone Test Match Score service in 1955. This rapidly became a hugely popular feature, but it is probably not well known that it was first proposed as early as 1948 when a Mr T. L. Geddes wrote the following to *The Times*:

Sir, Being a Scotsman, I have no interest in cricket. But at this season when all my mad English friends constantly ask me: 'Have you heard the latest score?' – to which question, obviously, I have neither the knowledge nor the desire to give an intelligent answer – I venture to suggest that the General Post Office might turn one of its golden-haired girls on to the job of providing a cricketing service for telephone subscribers. At the usual charge of 1d per call, my friends would then be able to dial CRI and obtain the score at any time of night or day.

The implementation of this suggestion would greatly increase my peace of mind, and that of all my compatriots similarly condemned to eke out a miserable, if somewhat more lucrative, existence among the extraordinary people who inhabit the southern portion of the island.

Other improvements at cricket matches included better wicket-drying equipment and more modern scoreboards, although the marvellous Trent Bridge building, which appeared in 1951, was never emulated by other clubs. Another example of cricket's slowness to recognize a new idea is the recently adopted use of light meters by umpires. As long ago as 1951 the editor of *Wisden* and several other writers were pointing out the logic of such an approach. Progress continues today, of course, with the Edgbaston ground covers, the endless new designs for bats, the use of helmets and, perhaps eventually, video replays for umpires. Artificial turf, at least for the outfield, will surely be suggested one day. Of one thing we can be sure – there will always be a strong lobby for resisting any change in cricket's traditions. And this is surely desirable, for in this way the best of the new ideas can be incorporated without resorting to wholesale change for its own sake as appeared to be the case during the Packer experiments.

3
Health and Wealth

County cricket has become too much of a business,
and too much of a money-making concern. There is, I
am afraid, very little real sport in it now as a game.
C. E. Green, writing in 1910

At least until very recently England has been the only cricket-playing country where the game is organized on wholly pro-fessional lines. As well as around 300 county players, a host of other people make their living from the game, including umpires, administrators, promotions organizers, groundsmen, coaches and league professionals. This full-time network to a certain extent justifies the claim that English first-class cricket is part of the entertainment industry. While it is true that in the other cricketing countries there are professional coaches and groundstaff, and that the leading players may receive generous payments for particular matches or tours, cricket is the main source of income for relatively few – certainly before the advent of the Packer-era in Australia. Cricket in the West Indies, New Zealand, India, etc., has never taken on the 'business' aspects of the English scene. It is for this reason that the health or well-being of English cricket has so often been described in purely financial terms. When the counties are profitable the game is said to be 'healthy', but when losses are incurred cricket is 'ailing'. This analogy to a business operation was carried to the extreme by the Political and Economic Planning (PEP) group, who, in 1956, published a study in which cricket was described as an industry 'fighting a losing battle against shortage of capital, shortage of income and shortage of the highly skilled labour the game requires'.

While it is true that the financial state of cricket can sometimes be linked to the quality or standard of play on the field, it is certainly not always the case. The economic climate of the country and other external forces may have a far greater influence on county profitability. This may indeed explain why so many of the minor changes made to the laws and conditions of cricket in the fifties, when finances were declining, failed to have any real beneficial effect.

This treatment of cricket as a business enterprise is taken for granted in the present post-Packer era where advertising, sponsorship and commercial planning are the key ingredients. This state has not been achieved overnight, however, but has developed from trends which were clearly discernible in the fifties and early sixties.

As in so many other aspects of the game, the social and economic climate of the post-war years had important and lasting repercussions on the financial structure of professional cricket. Also, in common with the other changes in cricket, the financial/business developments were not always well received. There was a strong body of opinion which regarded cricket as being above any sort of commercialism. As an example, the PEP study was controversial not only because of its contents – the imminent demise of cricket was predicted – but its very title, 'The Cricket Industry', did not sit well with some traditionalists who cherished 'the meadow game with the beautiful name'. It is doubtful whether even those who sounded warnings in the fifties foresaw the type of razzmatazz, violence and ill-feeling which the money factor has brought to much modern cricket (particularly in Australia), but clearly there was a great deal of concern. Equally, it can be argued that without a certain degree of commercialization cricket may never have recovered from the economic slump it experienced in the late fifties.

It would be wrong to imply that the 'sordid' influence of money has only been apparent in cricket since the last war. As long ago as the eighteenth century the 'great' games were played for unbelievably high stakes by the noblemen who patronized the game. Although accurate details are hard to find, more than 1000 guineas per game was often reported in contemporary accounts, a fortune by today's standards. Gambling among spectators, organizers and even players was also widespread well into the nineteenth century, and the leading bookmakers were a common sight in front of the pavilion at Lord's. Lord Frederick Beauclerk, one of the leading players, boasted of making at least 600 guineas a year from cricket bets. With so much money involved, trouble and scandal were inevitable and stories of matches being 'sold' by the leading players were commonplace. This was cricket's 'Dark

Chapter' described so vividly by William Beldham in Pycroft's classic book *The Cricket Field*. Eventually, in keeping with the trends of Victorian England, there was a purge which involved the banning of two leading players for corruption and the book-makers disappeared from the grounds. Mercifully, this was the last time that cricket was linked with bribery and match-fixing. Other sports, notably football and boxing, have not been so fortunate and perhaps the cynic would observe that, as more and more money comes into cricket, future scandals are inevitable. Let us hope not, although the recent events concerning Lillee, Marsh and Younis betting against their own sides do not augur well.

In the mid-nineteenth century money and cricket continued to go hand in hand, but now in a more commercial sense. William Clarke, an early cricket entrepreneur, made a fortune from his All-England Eleven and, indeed, money was at the root of the team's ultimate fragmentation into rival sides. The earliest overseas tours to America and Australia, although inspired by a sense of adventure, were also motivated by profit and the players and tour organizers often made quite large sums of money. When such tours were eventually taken over by central authorities – the MCC in 1903-4 and the Australian Board in 1909 — such profits could more readily be channelled back into cricket as a whole.

Throughout most of the twentieth century, therefore, cricket was essentially a non-commercial, non-profit-making under-taking. In the changing world after 1945, however, such a leisurely and haphazard approach to a professional entertainment (or industry) was hopelessly inappropriate. Before the war, cricket had managed to stay solvent while never exactly thriving, and this was perfectly acceptable since the professional players were comparatively well rewarded. Even during the Great Depression no county clubs went bankrupt, although many walked a tight-rope that usually relied on a local benefactor to bail them out. Why then, after surviving the worst of all economic disasters, did county cricket come perilously close to extinction in the late fifties, when the nation in general had apparently 'never had it so good'?

Some insight into this question can perhaps be gained by a consideration of the drastic changes that occurred in the balance sheets of the county clubs – changes that were largely dictated by forces outside the direct control of cricket itself. Firstly, on the income side there have traditionally been three major sources –

members' subscriptions, gate receipts and a share of the Test Match profits. Others that have recently become more important, such as sponsorship and lotteries, will be discussed later. Of the three, membership and Test Match income underwent a steady increase after the war while there was a corresponding decrease in gate receipts. The reason for this switch to membership was purely financial. For anyone attending even a few days play during the season membership made very good sense at the rates prevailing during the fifties and sixties. At the grounds which hosted Test Matches the outlay was worthwhile for that one match alone. So, while the counties benefited from a trend which ensured a stable lump sum income before the season started, they were in many cases underpricing their product. For example, the annual membership for the Hampshire Club was the same in 1951 as it had been in 1895 – just one guinea. In fact, it was not until the sixties that the subscription matched the three guineas that was paid by members of the Hambledon Club in 1791!

This situation was typical of most counties and probably arose from the complacency caused by high attendances during the late forties and early fifties – the initial post-war boom. Counties were wealthy for a few short years and saw no reason to set realistic membership fees. After all, they were not in the business of making a profit. Unfortunately, the boom did not last long and non-member attendance dropped off sharply. Figure 1 [see p. 42] depicts the total paying attendance at County Championship matches for each season between 1947 and 1963. The scatter of the points reflects the usual minor variations caused by the weather, but in general the downward trend is crystal clear.

The post-war boom, which lasted roughly until 1952, was an interesting phenomenon. Playing standards had yet to return to the pre-war level, Test Match success for England against Australia was virtually non-existent and there was a manpower crisis which demanded full employment, yet cricket attendances broke all records. From the informal season of Victory Tests in 1945, when nearly half a million people watched the matches at Lord's alone, the stage was set. The 'Test' over the Whitsun weekend established a record gate for a three-day game. The tour to Australia in 1946/7 brought previously unheard of profits and the Australian series of 1948 broke all attendance records. The County Championship was supported as it had never been before the war and reached a peak in the famous summer of 1947 – the year of Compton and Edrich. Sadly, however, the high attendances of these few years turned out to be a pinnacle from which there ensued a steady decline. By 1963 the number of people paying to see county matches had dropped by as much as two-thirds from the 1947 figure – a stunning turnaround. There were many who pointed to the fact that membership had doubled since before the war, but this alone could not account for the decline. It would have required every single member to have attended thirty days play each year for that to explain the drop.

Whichever way the figures are juggled the basic fact cannot be disputed that fewer and fewer people were willing or able to

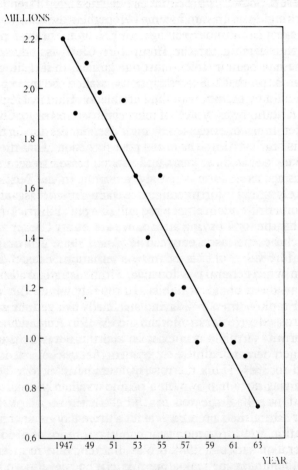

**Figure 1.   Paying attendance at County
Championship Matches.**

watch county cricket after the initial heady fling of the late forties. When viewed in the context of England's developing post-war social picture this should come as no surprise. Many of those who watched Compton, Edrich and the other pre-war favourites in 1947 were enjoying a free summer after demobilization from the forces. The fifties, however, were historically a period of very high employment in Great Britain, and few had time to watch mid-week cricket. The mood of post-war celebration necessarily gave way to a concentration on the more serious aspects of day-to-day life. As for the weekends and paid holidays, there were new interests to attract an increasingly affluent middle and working class. Figure 2 [see p. 44] depicts the rise of perhaps the two greatest influences on human activity in the post-war era, namely the dramatic increase in private motor cars and television sets. These were powerful counter-attractions to spending seven hours of a precious Saturday on a hard wooden bench, in unpredictable weather, watching cricket of an increasingly slow tempo. Although it is true that television also stimulated interest in cricket this influence really only fuelled the modern over-emphasis on Test Match cricket to the exclusion of other forms.

Cricket was not the only well-established entertainment to suffer, as the chart for cinema-going demonstrates. People were more likely to engage in a participative activity such as taking the family for a drive, sailing, playing golf or even club cricket.

Finally, the third major source of income for cricket and the county clubs was, and remains today, the share in Test Match profits. The value of this contribution naturally depends very much on which country is touring, with Australia traditionally being way ahead of everyone else. In 1963, however, the famous tour by Frank Worrell's West Indians finally bridged the gap and in fact grossed a greater profit than did the 1961 Australian series. The enormity of this was not lost on the counties, who promptly re-arranged the schedules to ensure that the West Indians returned in 1966. This increase in attendance at West Indian matches was not only by virtue of a marvellously entertaining team but was also affected by the changing social picture in post-war Britain. The fifties saw a tremendous increase in immigration from Commonwealth countries and by 1963 there were over a quarter of a million West Indians resident in Britain, most of them near the major Test Match centres. They not only helped to increase attendances but brought a new gaiety and life to the Test scene.

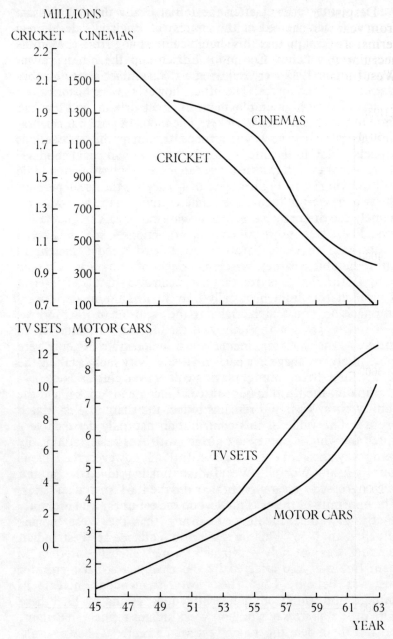

MILLIONS

CRICKET   CINEMAS

CINEMAS

CRICKET

TV SETS   MOTOR CARS

TV SETS

MOTOR CARS

YEAR

**Figure 2.   Above – The decline in cricket and
cinema attendance.
Below – The increase in TV sets
and motor cars.**

Despite the fact that Test Match profits were not consistent from year to year, they did at least show a steady increase, in real terms, as illustrated in Figure 3 [see below]. Here the profits accruing to a Test Match host county are plotted for Australian, West Indian and South African years. The Australian tours were

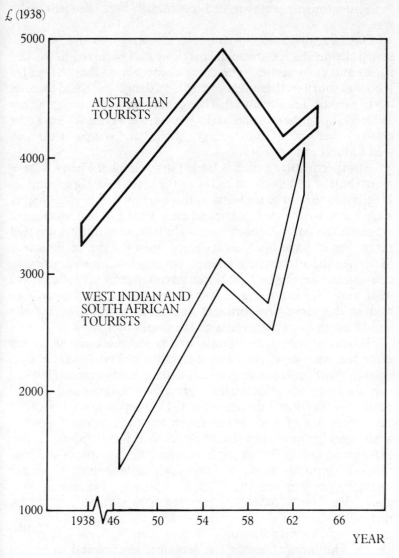

Figure 3.   Test Match profits to counties (T.M.)

clearly more profitable with the other two countries roughly equivalent. The curves are plotted in constant 1938 pounds and are therefore adjusted for inflation. It is clear, therefore, that this source of revenue was becoming more and more important for the counties compared to other income. In this respect it was fortunate, or perhaps essential, that there were no blank years – without a touring team – as had occasionally happened before the war.

One warning note to county treasurers, however, was the sharp dip in the Test Match share-out that occurred in the late fifties and early sixties. The curve clearly shows that, no matter who was touring, these years signalled a dangerous trend towards lower profits. Throughout this book these same few years, roughly 1957-61, appear again and again as a period of crisis for cricket: a crisis in behaviour, controversy, quality and tempo of play, as well as financial viability.

Another feature which is buried in the data of Figure 3 is the contribution of television rights to the total Test Match profits. Negligible up to the mid-fifties, this portion had become highly significant by the early sixties when at least £40,000 was shared amongst the counties each season. In fact, without this windfall there would have been no recovery from the dip in Figure 3. Whether the increased television coverage was instrumental in causing the decline in Test Match attendance from the heights of 1948 and 1953 is uncertain. If so, at least it paid for the privilege and at the same time brought cricket-watching to many who would never have bothered with the game otherwise.

To summarize, the income trends for professional cricket after the war were rising membership and Test Match profits, coupled with falling county championship gate receipts. How did this measure up to expenses – principally salaries and ground maintenance? For a decade after 1945 everything went well. In fact, there was a sufficient surplus among most counties to enable ambitious ground and facilities improvements to be made. Edgbaston shines out as the most dramatic example of this, the modern ground becoming unrecognizable from the rather ordinary pre-war version. With a surprising suddenness, however, the county balance sheets began to take on a distinctly unhealthy look. Talk of some county clubs going bankrupt was not as wild as many thought at the time. Figure 4 [see p. 47] shows the annual profit or loss for two typical counties: Leicestershire and Gloucestershire. The change in character as

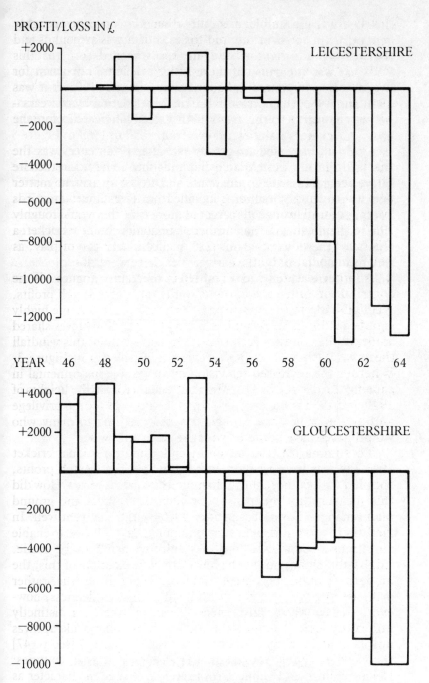

Figure 4. Annual profit/loss figures for two counties in the post-war era.

the post-war era unfolded is quite dramatic. The warning signs generally appeared in the mid-fifties, but it was around 1958 – that year again – that the floodgates really opened.

What was the cause of these sudden deficits? Certainly this was a period of general inflation (approximately 100% between 1946 and 1963) in contrast to the mainly deflationary conditions before the war, and this resulted in a steady increase in running costs. Cricketers' salaries, shown from 1890 to 1963 in Figure 5 [see below], increased at a greater rate after 1945 than ever before but still did not quite match this inflation. (The figures on the curve are necessarily approximate and are for an average capped county player, not including income from Tests, tours, etc.) The average county wage bill increased more than this would indicate due to the decline in the number of amateurs. Immediately after the war there were about 220 professionals playing in the championship but by the early sixties there were closer to 300, a 36% increase which had a real effect on county finances. This,

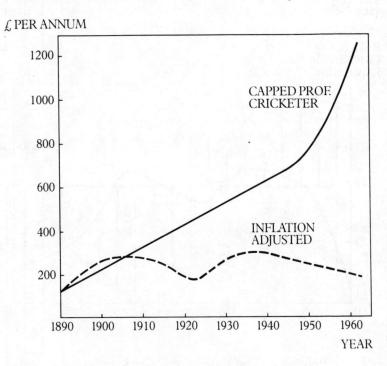

**Figure 5.   Professional Cricketers' salaries –
long term view.**

coupled with the falling attendances, failure to increase entrance and membership fees, and a general complacency, resulted in the dramatic trend towards financial disaster for all but a few counties.

The precarious balance of county finances was demonstrated in 1952 when the Chancellor of the Exchequer, R. A. Butler, introduced an increase in Entertainment Tax. This would have meant most counties finding an extra one to two thousand pounds each year, and many were afraid of bankruptcy. Hampshire took the immediate step of leaving the Minor Counties Competition in order to cut costs. Eventually, as a result of pressure from MCC and a group of Labour Members of Parliament (an unusual alliance), cricket clubs were exempted from the Chancellor's scheme. Clearly, it had not yet been decided whether cricket was an entertainment or not!

What of the cricketers' personal finances? We have already shown (Figure 5) [see p. 48] how salaries have changed over the years, but perhaps a more informative curve is given in Figure 6 [see below]. Here, the ratio of the cricketer's salary ('average'

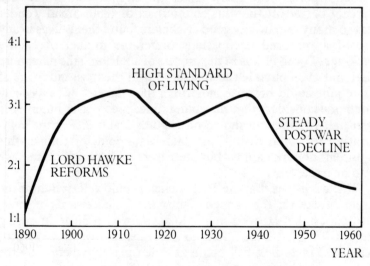

Figure 6. The Professional Cricketer's salary relative to an unskilled labourer – long term view.

capped player) to that of an unskilled labourer is shown between the years 1890 and 1963. The figures again are largely an estimate based on several sources but the overall trends are probably accurate. Before the Golden Age, a county cricketer was only rewarded marginally above the unskilled labourer and was clearly not in the same category as a craftsman, farmer or teacher. This situation was greatly improved in the years leading up to the first war, largely through the initiative of Lord Hawke and the Yorkshire club who were instrumental in dramatically improving the lot of the professional. Lord Harris and C. W. Alcock also played a significant part. Winter pay and post-retirement schemes helped to reduce the incidence of hardship and even the occasional suicide amongst cricketers of the period. The result was that right up to the outbreak of the second war the cricketer typically enjoyed three times the income of an unskilled labourer and was able to boast a certain financial and social standing in the community. He earned as much as a typical Civil Service executive. He was not wealthy but, compared to other opportunities open to a fourteen-year-old school-leaver, cricket was a highly desirable profession. All this changed after the war when the cricketer's relative salary slipped almost as rapidly as it had risen during the Golden Age. By the early sixties the capped county pro was scarcely better off than his counterpart of 1890. Small wonder that so many potentially good cricketers found themselves in any one of a hundred occupations preferable to that of county cricketer. Football was in the process of abolishing the maximum wage but even outside the sporting world the most mundane of office jobs could promise more than the cricket field; especially when one considers that the young, uncapped player might only earn half the income shown on Figures 5 and 6. For the comparative few who made Test Match stardom, of course, this argument does not apply, but these were such a small percentage as to be irrelevant.

While it is true that the Test cricketer could at least double the figures given for the capped county man, the rewards of international cricket failed dismally to keep up with inflation during the period. The 1946/7 tour to Australia was worth £825 plus expenses (including full bonus) to each player, whereas by the early sixties this had only risen to around £1000 plus expenses. The value of the pound had halved in this same period. For domestic Test Matches the picture was similar. Between 1947 and 1963 the players' rate of compensation was only raised once –

from £15 per day to £20. All this during a period when the profits from Test Matches were increasing dramatically even after the effects of inflation. The conditions which fostered the takeover by Packer were being firmly set in place throughout the fifties.

In one respect, however, the post-war player was significantly better off than his predecessors: the benefit. The huge crowds of the immediate post-war years produced record tax-free sums for the star names like Compton (£12,000 in 1949) and Washbrook (£14,000 in 1948). A 'friendly' Roses match in 1945 brought over £8000 in memory of the late Hedley Verity. All this compared with the record pre-war figure of £4016 for Roy Kilner of Yorkshire, itself worth about £8000 in 1948 pounds. For the average pro it was still a perilously hit-or-miss affair, of course, but the benefit gradually assumed greater importance as the normal county salary was eroded in true value. What had previously just been a benefit 'match' became a benefit 'year' or 'fund'. A committee was usually set up to help the player organize Sunday matches, show-business events and a host of other innovative schemes which are now considered commonplace. Every attempt was needed to squeeze each last penny from the cricketer's 'last chance'.

For the precious few 'star' cricketers there were increasing opportunities to supplement their regular income with advertising and writing. In the boom years straight after the war Denis Compton was probably the most marketable property in English sport. An international footballer as well as the most entertaining cricketer of the day, his face, or rather his hair, became synonymous with Brylcreem. It is interesting to compare the different contributions to Compton's income during his heyday. After the war he was signed to a three-year contract by Middlesex which was worth between five and six hundred pounds a year with all travel and hotel expenses paid. For some cricketers this would be their only significant income. During a season like 1948, however, Compton would have supplemented this by perhaps £400 through Test matches and the Gentlemen versus Players game. A winter tour was also quite lucrative, the one to Australia in 1946/7 being worth £825 plus expenses to the professionals. When the reported payment for the Brylcreem ads of £1200 per year is included then an annual income of about £3000 is probably not an unreasonable estimate. Good money indeed, but only for a precious few. Certainly in a case like Compton's, nobody could argue that it was not richly deserved. It is perhaps indicative, though, of the way in which cricket was heading that county cricket was the least important financial contribution for Compton, with Test Matches and advertising far outweighing it. On top of all this, of course, came that benefit of over £12,000 in 1949. For many players, however, a more modest benefit of around £2000 was hardly a huge reward for a career of maybe twenty or twenty-five years.

By 1963 the rewards had hardly kept pace with the increased cost of living. The county salary had probably doubled to about £1000. The Test and representative fees had hardly changed, say £550 per season for an England regular. The Australian tour was worth £1100. The most lucrative advertising contracts, like Compton's with Brylcreem, were now more likely to go to a footballer, and anyway there was no professional with the mass appeal and popularity of Compton. Ken Barrington, writing in 1963, felt it was impossible for even the top two or three professionals to earn more than £4000 in their best year. That may seem a lot compared to a labourer but here we are talking about the two or three individuals in the world who are at the very pinnacle of their profession. Hardly comparable to an Arnold Palmer, a Ken Rosewall, or a Lester Piggott.

Clearly, from this detailed account of the rapidly deteriorating financial state of county cricket, something had to be done. The simple answers, and the ones which eventually led to a renascence in cricket's fortunes, were Supporters' Clubs, sponsorship and the introduction of one-day, limited-overs cricket.

The growth of the Supporters' Club was truly a feature of the fifties. Worcestershire had introduced a football pool scheme during the winter of 1949 and Charles Palmer took the idea with him when he moved from that county to Leicestershire the following year. There, things began to grow rapidly. After six months a cheque for £2000 was presented to the club, and by the end of 1953 £20,000 had been raised. Meanwhile, similar Supporters' Clubs had sprung up in Glamorgan and Warwickshire, and soon all these pioneering counties were receiving a substantial supplementary income. The main money-making activity of these clubs was a shilling-a-week football pool, utilizing club volunteers as agents, and made possible by recent legislation.

Eventually all the other counties followed suit with the traditionalists Yorkshire finally succumbing in 1964. There had been a feeling among some of the diehards that even such apparently harmless commercial ventures had no place in cricket.

The case of Glamorgan provides a good example. Their Supporters' Club was formed in 1952, which happened to be exactly the last year in which the county were able to balance expenditure against income from truly cricket sources. In the years which followed, the football pool proceeds were vital to the continuation of a viable club but, as Wilfred Wooller describes, the idea was not immediately welcomed:

> The principle . . . was the subject of some fine rhetoric in the ACCC at Lord's. Cricket (we gathered from certain aloof sources) was on the slippery path to hell. The academic solemnity of the discussions was intriguing. However, meetings at national headquarters were a picnic compared with the Calvinistic religious revival which took place during the winter of 1951 among the Glamorgan full committee. John Wesley would indeed have been proud of the oratory and fervour.

Nevertheless, the Club was eventually started and became an instant success. At its peak as much as £32,000 per year was being donated to the county which was in danger of becoming rich beyond anyone's wildest dreams. The market shrank somewhat when the 1956 Betting Act legalized the small lottery, and the subsequent proceeds became more like £6000-£8000 including bingo and prize draws.

This story is similar to that in many other counties. Large profits to begin with, followed by a good steady income which came to be relied on for balancing the books. Some counties instituted long-overdue ground and amenity improvements, but by the late fifties the Supporters' Club donations were no longer enough to offset the increasingly large operating losses of most counties. At Warwickshire, of course, the scheme became larger and more lucrative than anywhere else, and was partially responsible for the transformation of Edgbaston as well as many generous donations outside the county.

Another big change in the financing of cricket was the increased contribution of sponsorship. This did not occur on the scale we have seen in the seventies or eighties, but the trend was unmistakably apparent. Not that sponsorship was new to cricket. Many of the earliest matches in the eighteenth century were promoted by the local public house or catering firm which made a considerable profit from the enterprise. The earliest international tours were privately sponsored either by individuals or a company like Spiers and Pond, the caterers, who organized the first tour to Australia after Charles Dickens had withdrawn from a planned speaking tour. In its earlier days cricket did not have a problem with being recognized as a commercial endeavour. It was only more recently that the game came to be regarded with a sanctity or reverence in which commercialism had no part to play. This attitude was on the part of the spectators and administrators, of course, rather than the players. While that extreme may have been unrealistic, the modern trend towards American-style packaging and the influence of 'big money' is equally distasteful to many.

During the interwar years sponsorship existed but in a far more subtle form than we know today. Many counties were kept afloat by a local patron, but he really took the form of a benefactor rather than true sponsorship. There was no profit motive for the sponsor. Sir Julian Cahn spent a fortune on cricket between the wars, financing his own team in matches against tourists, clubs, leagues and other sides. He also sponsored overseas tours and was responsible for bringing Test stars like Dempster, Walsh and Jackson to county cricket. Again, this was not direct sponsorship but it certainly was of material benefit to a county like Leicestershire.

One of the earliest post-war examples of true sponsorship concerned the tremendous assistance given to Northamptonshire by the local company, British Timken. In conjunction with a thriving Supporters' Club, they contributed in many ways, including ground improvements, and were partially responsible for the recruitment of so many experienced players from outside the county. Overseas players like George Tribe, Jock Livingston and Jack Manning were instrumental in revolutionizing their fortunes on the field of play. From a Cinderella team they became a force to be reckoned with. Other recruits included Freddie Brown, Albert Nutter, Norman Oldfield, Des Barrick, Fred Jakeman, Frank Tyson and Raman Subba Row, many of them employed by Timken. This activity was not without a certain amount of opposition, especially from outside the county, but the results were undoubtedly beneficial and have clearly encouraged the subsequent development of local talent rather than the reverse.

Gradually throughout the period similar examples of sponsorship began to break into county cricket. Some of the leading amateur cricketers could even be regarded as being sponsored by their employer, who often gained prestige or advertising from the services of a famous sports personality. It was not until the introduction of the long-awaited knock-out competition in 1963, however, that sponsorship as we know it today finally became a comprehensive part of the first-class cricket scene. The history of the introduction of one-day cricket is dealt with in the next chapter, but one of the main driving forces for its inception was the dramatic fall in attendances described above. The opportunity to attract considerable revenue through sponsorship was really an added bonus that materialized after the tournament had been conceived. At first the income from Gillette was modest – £6500 in the first year – and was only designed to provide a guarantee against possible losses. Soon, however, the commercial participation escalated and was followed in the later sixties by a succession of lucrative cricket sponsorship deals throughout the world. Rothmans introduced their Cavaliers team to be followed by John Player, Benson & Hedges, Prudential, Schweppes and others. Of these, Rothmans really were the first and their efforts truly had the interest of the game at heart. It was a shame that their exit from English cricket sponsorship was tinged with acrimony over the Sunday TV issue. Much valuable work was also done to foster cricket in New Zealand and the West Indies by the Shell Oil Company. Today, of course, sponsorship is taken for granted, and, although its presence may be regretted by some, it is as well to remember that professional cricket might have all but died without it.

To summarize, the financial development of the period was characterized initially by ambitious expansionist policies in the counties – better grounds, more professionals, overseas recruits – fuelled by high post-war attendances and new Supporters' Club revenues. There followed a sudden reversal in profitability, the professional suffered a serious decline in relative remuneration, and the future was distinctly questionable. By 1963, however, all of the developments which would rescue the game's finances were securely in place. One-day games, sponsorship, more Test matches and the rise of West Indian cricket were about to launch a far more prosperous era despite the continued erosion of grass-roots attendances at county matches.

4

Brighter Cricket

The trend set in motion during the fifties and early sixties – sponsorship, one-day cricket, overseas players, extreme professionalism, etc. — were more than just a passing fashion. They have gained momentum to such an extent that the innovations and whims of those days now dominate the game of today. The financial side of cricket, described already in terms of the prevailing social climate, provides some rationale for the changes brought about during those pivotal years in the game's history. Now, though, an attempt must be made to study the other factors which dictated change, to analyze the contemporary perceptions regarding cricket. Up to now we have catalogued developments in the cold terms of profit and loss, of attendances and salaries, but cricket is an athletic activity and this story should now return to the field of play.

The conventional wisdom regarding the mood of Britain during the first two post-war decades is that there was a general feeling of dissatisfaction with the status quo. There was an unspoken feeling that 'things' should be better than they were. While this is probably to a certain extent true of any period, it was a natural enough result of the war and the austerity years which followed. The general public wanted progress and change in every aspect of their lives and by the time the economic boom of the fifties came along many of these material desires were indeed being fulfilled. Everyone wanted better jobs, higher wages, better education, social services for their families, indeed a steady stream of the comforts of life. A similar thirst for progress would appear to have been the prime mover in the development of cricket.

Every summer seemed to bring a chorus of appeals for 'better' cricket. 'Better than what' was not always defined. Certainly there were faults with the game in the fifties. Defensiveness flourished as never before and there was a dull uniformity about cricket that had not been the case before the war. The contemporary criticism was usually vague and ill-defined, but somehow there just had to be something better, or in the word of the time 'brighter'. The term 'brighter cricket' seems hopelessly inappropriate for a game of such endless subtlety and skill but it was a phrase invoked ad nauseam during the fifties. The word 'bright' suggests a shallow and superficial tinselling of cricket, and this is precisely what resulted with the evolution of the Sunday league and – the ultimate in gaudiness – the Packer pyjama games.

This general feeling of dissatisfaction with cricket gave birth to the modern trend of setting up committees to inquire into the 'welfare of the game'. Identifying these by the name of the chairman we had the Findlay (1937), Jackson (1944), Altham (1957), Rait Kerr/Ashton (1961) and Clark (1966) committees; all set up by the MCC at the request of the counties. In addition, the Political and Economic Planning study (PEP, 1956) was a similar, if non-establishment, investigation. In truth, these committees, hard-working and well-meaning though they were, achieved comparatively little in the way of meaningful progress with the very real exception of the Rait Kerr/Ashton report which will be discussed later.

While both the pre-war Findlay commission and the 1944 Jackson committee had recognized the poor financial health of county cricket, they had wholeheartedly rejected any change of structure. Even at this early stage, however, they did at least discuss such innovative suggestions as Sunday play, a two-divisional system, fewer first-class counties, limited-overs or limited-time for first innings, and a knock-out tournament. These ideas are not as modern as many would believe, but the actual implementation of any of them was considered too radical at that time.

By the early fifties, however, the familiar cry of 'brighter cricket' was beginning to make itself heard. The press carried charts showing the decline in run scoring rates, the number of sixes being hit and so on. Trophies and prizes were awarded for feats such as the fastest hundred and a 'Brighter Cricket Table' was instituted in the *News Chronicle* (Essex, as if to answer Trevor Bailey's critics, were the first winners in 1952). Each year the pleas for more enterprise grew louder and louder. As early as 1951 Sir Home Gordon made the following prophetic statement:

First-class cricket is standing at the parting of the ways. Is it to maintain its tremendous and deserved popularity or is it to fade into dreary occupation of the wicket, which will keep spectators away in increasing numbers? The imminent crisis is financial.

A quick survey of *Wisden* during the fifties also gives a flavour of the prevalent mood. The 1952 issue contained a typical cross-section of comments. Col. R. S. Rait Kerr called for 'more enterprise' in county cricket, citing the fact that 50% of matches in 1951 were drawn, compared to only 25% in 1947. This, it was claimed, had caused the decrease in attendance. The trend towards defensive and unentertaining play was bemoaned in an article by Neville Cardus entitled 'A Call For Culture: Safety First Can Ruin Cricket'. The notes by the editor contained a discussion of the 'Causes Of Listless Cricket'. In 1954 the editor regretfully acknowledged the accuracy of Home Gordon's insidious new phrase – 'occupation of the crease' – to characterize the dull play that was prevalent. The following year the evil of time-wasting was noted and the blame for cricket's ills was put squarely on the shoulders of the professional and his supposed safety-conscious attitude: 'The approach of the professional player is responsible for the alarming fall in attendance as well as for the lack of success of the English professional batsman in Test cricket.'

Diana Rait Kerr (the Colonel's daughter and a noted historian) has pointed out the importance of this defensive state of mind in the cricket of the fifties, and that this may have been related to the socio-economic conditions of the period:

> The game was gripped to the point of suffocation in an iron band imposed by the gospel of containment, shackling the players so that they could not break out of their prison even if they would. Never had a leaven of lightness and joy been more sorely needed, for, while there had been times in the past when cricket had been in the doldrums and survived, dullness had never before been allied in quite the same way with social and economic pressures.

The *Cricketer* added another unkind but accurate condemnation: 'Cricket has become a sullen, unhappy business and not a successful business either!'

The lack of entertainment value in cricket of the fifties was often linked to the decline in available, talented amateur players, to be documented in a later chapter. While this was certainly a significant contributory factor, the argument was occasionally twisted in order to denigrate the contributions of the game's professionals. In some quarters, as we have seen, all sorts of measures were suggested to artificially keep amateurs in the game while professionals were depicted as selfishly reducing cricket to a business and adopting safety-first tactics. This argument owed more to the remnants of class distinction still apparent in the England of those days than to fact. There were dull amateurs and attractive professionals to prove the point. As we have discussed, a more significant reason for the dull play of the period was probably the poor quality of the pitches being prepared by most of the counties.

Of course, as one looks back on the cricket of the fifties and recalls the glorious play of Graveney, May and Compton, the attacking and vital captaincy of Surridge, Wooller and others, it is natural to question all this talk of defensive, unentertaining cricket. While it is true that there were marvellous players in the game, time inevitably adds a filter to our memories such that the many occasions when these batsmen were left prodding away on a lifeless spinners' wicket are forgotten. The attendance figures told the true story, however, and in 1956, while Laker and Lock were stifling batsmen on pitches that would have eventually killed cricket as an entertainment, the Political and Economic Planning group published their study of *The Cricket Industry*.

The main remedy put forward by the PEP report was the idea of only playing first-class cricket at weekends, including Sunday play. The PEP rationale for this was that attendances at mid-week games were low and that less cricket would bring zest back into the game. The same idea had been put forward in 1949 by J. Daniell, the former Somerset captain, and was to be resurrected several times by Ronnie Aird, the MCC secretary. These proposals, however, were aimed at bringing the amateur player back to county cricket. None of these people seemed to realize the enormity of their suggestion. In effect they would have totally disassembled the professional game by discouraging county membership, a point that was quickly raised at the time by the county secretaries who recognized the realities of economic life. As Brian Castor, the Surrey secretary, put it, 'The mid-week games make money by virtue of the invisible presence of 10,000 members.' The cost of keeping up the ground is independent of the number of games, so the idea of 'weekends only' has never been implemented, yet it will doubtless be raised again and again in the future.

Another reason why the PEP report was not well received in cricket's administrative circles was that this group of 'intellectual' outsiders dared to criticize MCC. There were allegations that MCC and the counties were organized on a basis of class distinction and snobbery, and that this resulted in an aversion to increased commercialization of cricket. This raised the hackles of many in the so-called 'establishment', but it is interesting to record how prophetic the PEP report was in many ways. Cricket in the seventies and eighties found it necessary to fully embrace commercial interests and the administration of the game has been opened to a far broader class of people, including ex-professional cricketers, just as suggested by PEP.

Despite the reservations about PEP, the MCC immediately instituted their own official investigation into the state of cricket. The Altham committee identified the causes of defensive cricket to be leg-side bowling, slow spinners' pitches, and a lower over-rate. Apart from some fine words about speeding up the tempo, the only significant committee recommendation that was instituted involved limiting the number of leg-side fielders to five in order to discourage negative bowling. Two radical suggestions, a limitation of the first innings to eighty-five overs and a trial knockout competition, were rejected by the counties.

By the time we entered the sixties, however, it was clear that the Altham measures had had little impact and that the financial plight of the counties was at crisis point. Added to this the play was getting even more dull – the medium-paced seam bowlers had inherited the earth – and the innovations of Altham were recognized as having been merely superficial details. What was needed was a major overhaul. In November 1960, a new committee was called for, to investigate the 'Structure of First-Class Cricket'. This was generally welcomed with a howl of indifference, for the public and the press had seen too many committees. It was not known at the time, however, that this one was to have a more lasting effect than all the others put together. In January 1961, the constitution of the committee, under the chairmanship of Colonel R. S. Rait Kerr, was announced and surprisingly included two professionals – Bill Bowes and Alec Bedser – both highly respected and level-headed.

In March 1961, before the actual question of structure had been considered, the committee issued a memorandum for the ACCC. This concerned solely the attitudes of cricketers, a sure sign that this was perceived as the real cause of cricket's ills rather than 'structure'. The counties were asked to put their own house in order by dropping dull performers and persevering with entertainers. Further, the county selectors should closely watch scoring-rates and county secretaries were charged with the duty of talking to groundsmen about producing fast, true pitches. Was this just the habitual lip-service or the beginnings of a real crusade? The county captains weighed in with a statement regarding their 'determination to provide entertaining cricket' and to 'increase the tempo'. All good stuff, but so often the enthusiasm of a cosy, pre-season meeting at Lord's can be lost once the cold winds of May are blowing across the cricket fields.

There were other factors at work, however, during this year of 1961. The Australians, under the captaincy of Richie Benaud, arrived on English shores direct from their historic series with Worrell's West Indians. The tied Test Match, the tickertape parade, the huge crowds and record gate receipts were still fresh in the mind as Benaud pledged attacking, positive cricket. England played their part and the on-the-field action began to match the committee-room rhetoric. As the *Cricketer* put it: 'The opportunity for action is here now, in 1961, and if it is missed it may not recur in time to save first-class cricket from further and very serious decline.' Even the County Championship played its part that year with Hampshire winning in fine style under the inspired and daring captaincy of A. D. C. Ingleby-Mackenzie. With Roy Marshall perhaps the finest attacking batsman in the country, they helped make the season a threshold for the new era to come.

Refreshing though the impact of Benaud, Worrell and Dexter was on cricket, it was the much maligned administrators who, towards the end of 1961, finally gave the game its most far-reaching jolt. After Rait Kerr's death, Sir Hubert Ashton, hero of the 1921 season and now the MP for Chelmsford, took over as chairman of the Committee of Enquiry. Under his guidance, two major recommendations were made: the introduction of a Knockout Cup and the start of Sunday play. Although these were considered to be important suggestions at the time, nobody could have forecast the dramatic long-term effects both ideas would have on the game.

The Times, in a leading article, wrote: 'What the melancholy experience of recent years has shown to the satisfaction of everyone except some nostalgic optimists is that the old order is visibly dying on its feet.' Some counties – Warwickshire, Glamorgan,

Worcestershire, Leicestershire, Northamptonshire among them – were healthy, of course, but others were perilously close to extinction. As well as the finances, the quality of play was in a state of atrophy. The twin solutions of knockout tournament and Sunday play were certainly to see a dramatic improvement in the financial side, and while their effect on the standard of play may be arguable, the tempo and urgency have definitely been uplifted.

In contrast to the quotes earlier cited from *Wisden* during the early to mid-fifties, by 1961 it was possible to find an article by Jack Fingleton entitled, 'Cricket Alive Again'. In 1962 Norman Preston could write, 'I have been watching Test cricket for forty years and I cannot recall a more pleasant atmosphere.' After the 1963 West Indian tour to England the Lord Mayor of London bade Worrell's team farewell with the description, 'A gale of change blowing through the hallowed halls of cricket.' Worrell's contribution to this uplifting of cricket cannot be overstated and his reward of a knighthood at the end of 1963 has seldom been more deserved. He had been appointed the first black captain of a West Indian touring team (for the 1960/61 tour to Australia) only after a long and bitter campaign in which the writer, C.L.R. James, was a leading figure. After all the publicity and acrimony, Worrell's actual captaincy could have been an anticlimax but instead was revolutionary. The flamboyant West Indian players were welded into a team as never before and became both effective and exciting to watch. The same group of players, under Alexander's captaincy, had been dull and negative against England just the previous winter. That tour to Australia and the followup to England in 1963 really set cricket enthusiasts buzzing again as they had not done since Compton and Bradman's immediate post-war heyday.

Richie Benaud also played his part, against Worrell and during the 1961 series in England. Always an attractive cricketer himself, he captained Australia in the traditional hard fashion but never in a dull, purely defensive way. An intelligent man, as shown by his television commentaries, he realized that the needs of the spectator were as important as the task of avoiding defeat. So many during the fifties had played as if nobody was watching with the natural result that pretty soon hardly anybody was. The Australian sides of the mid-fifties had been rather dull but Benaud had the same effect as Worrell. Not that fast scoring was the key ingredient; in the historic series with the West Indians, Australia scored at the very slow rate of 38 runs per 100 balls, but the play was vital and aggressive. The 1958/59 tour by England was largely lost through the different attitudes brought to the series – attrition by England and aggression by Benaud's Australia.

Not all the key figures in the revitalization of cricket were on the field of play. Nobody in post-war cricket symbolized enterprise and dynamism more than Walter Robins, first as a player for Middlesex but equally importantly as an administrator. The prime of his playing career had been before the war, when he made all of his nineteen appearances for England, but he reappeared to lead Middlesex to the championship in 1947 with some typically aggressive batting, bowling, fielding and captaincy. His partnership with Compton and Edrich was unstoppable. Robins was a magnetic, charming and entertaining character but most significant was his desire to dominate proceedings. In his role as cricket administrator this was clearly his intention. After that disastrous 1958/59 MCC tour to Australia, Robins emerged as the leading figure in a campaign to improve the quality and demeanour of England's cricketers and the attractiveness and vitality of their play. The following winter he was chosen as manager of the MCC tour to the West Indies.

The last tour there, under Hutton in 1953/54, had been a stormy affair with team discipline a major problem, and the MCC were determined that this would not be repeated. The older generation of strong-willed and self-confident players were discarded and a largely new team was sent under Robins' very tight rein. The senior players – May and Cowdrey particularly – may have found him erratic, too dictatorial and difficult to cope with. No doubt his military-style discipline was effective in avoiding the type of excesses attributed to some of the junior players on the previous tour, but to people of the experience, intelligence and culture of May and Cowdrey it was, apparently, irksome. Robins had a caustic tongue and was not renowned for his tact. 'Extraordinary histrionics of our manager' is how Cowdrey described Robins' general behaviour and, indeed, the pair were to have an ugly confrontation on the last day of the tour.

The story runs as follows. England had fought their way to a 1-0 lead in the series before entering the final Test without May and Statham, who had returned to England, and with several other front-line players nursing ailments and general weariness after a gruelling tour. The intense heat, long travel and endless barrage of intimidatory fast bowling has usually made the West Indian tour far from the Caribbean holiday it might sound.

Anyway, against all the odds Cowdrey, the stand-in captain, led England to a draw in this final game, thereby clinching the first ever series win by an English touring side in the West Indies. (Since then Cowdrey repeated the trick in 1967/68 and remains the only successful captain.) Entering the final day of the tour there was still a chance for a West Indian victory if England's last four wickets collapsed, but Parks and Mike Smith put on a marvellous display and the game drifted to an honourable draw. Honourable, that is, to most Englishmen except Walter Robins. Alan Ross, the *Observer*'s correspondent, describes events perfectly:

> Some would have liked Cowdrey to declare but there was precious little point in squandering 29 days' hard graft on a spree for a sprinkling of spectators. . . . An earlier declaration in such circumstances could only have been nominal, if not downright foolish. Yet, on what should have been an afternoon of celebration, the manager chose to rebuke the England captain in unnecessarily crude terms before his team and to dissociate himself from the whole proceedings. I hope he has repented, though I doubt whether repentence comes easily to him.

The incident certainly left Cowdrey saddened and over the years he became convinced that it also cost him the England captaincy once Robins was made Chairman of the Selectors in 1962. Perhaps, though, there were other reasons for Robins' erratic behaviour. E.W. Swanton writes: 'Most of us grow mellower, I suppose, with age, but poor Walter became if anything rather less so; in retrospect these early years of the 60s must have seen the first onset of the hardening of the brain arteries which after a long and particularly distressing illness proved fatal in 1968.'

Ian Peebles, who covered this West Indian tour as a correspondent, and was a close friend of Robins, has confirmed that he was 'much troubled by high blood pressure at this moment and easily upset'.

Despite the occasional overzealousness of Robins' fervour he was probably just the force English cricket needed at this time. His influence became even greater when, in 1962, he was appointed as Chairman of the Selectors. He immediately called a meeting of the press to launch his campaign. (Robins' diligence in giving reporters the utmost co-operation has been remarked on many times and for this reason he usually received a good press himself.) The gist of his message was plain enough: 'Cricketers must play aggressively at all times, otherwise they will not be chosen for England.' He added that he 'would not mind losing all five Tests in Australia if we played the right way'. Stirring stuff, but how far removed from the hard, businesslike cricket scene of the 1980s.

There is no doubt that Robins was absolutely right in his insistence on more aggression. John Woodcock summed up the reasons as follows:

> By and large there is probably, in terms of entertainment, no great difference between England's cricket these last five years and a lot of their cricket in the hazier past. . . But with the development of the welfare state and the privileges it provides, the spectator is more particular than he was. He has come to demand a fuller flavour for his money.

This is an important point but there were social forces in addition to the welfare state and its privileges that influenced this demand for 'brighter' cricket. If the forties had been largely drab and the fifties were a decade of steady economic improvement, then the sixties were a time of flair and excitement in the social life of England. The society of the sixties was not only more affluent but also culturally more permissive. It was a time of mini-skirts and the Beatles, of Carnaby Street and cannabis. The range of leisure activities was so great that any that were not 'bright' would fall by the wayside – certainly as far as the emerging generation was concerned. Cricket was not the only traditional sport to suffer in this way. Soccer had to fight just as hard to hold off the challenge of golf, climbing, sailing and other 'modern' participatory and individual sports.

Returning to the conduct of the game, despite the worthy rhetoric of Walter Robins and the deeds of Worrell and company, it was, as we have said, the administrators who really engineered the ultimate in making professional cricket an activity that fitted the modern England. They finally, in 1963, introduced a knock-out competition, the following year named the Gillette Cup.

This innovation was certainly not a snap decision but came after a long history of attempts to institute a knock-out tournament. The first proposals came as long ago as 1855, long before there was a County Championship, but they came to nothing. In 1873 the MCC actually instituted a county knock-out competition, but after much argument only two counties participated, one match was played, and the idea was dropped. In December 1903, C.B. Fry, then at the height of his athletic fame and always an original thinker, sent a detailed circular to all the counties urging a cricket competition along the lines of the FA Cup. Although there was support from five of the counties, the majority were against because of the possible disruption of the, by then established, championship. W.A. Bettesworth typified the establishment reaction to Fry's radical proposals: 'The idea of cups is abhorrent to about ninety-nine cricketers out of a hundred ... There are heaps of objections to the proposed scheme and it is difficult to think of anything in its favour.'

This effectively squashed the idea for another forty years until, as we have seen, the climate at the end of the war prompted the Advisory County Cricket Committee to set up a group to devise a knock-out tournament. In March 1945 the group of four county secretaries and Colonel Rait Kerr, Secretary of the MCC, disclosed a proposal for 'The Cricket Cup' to be played for in the first season after the war. They suggested that the seventeen counties play a series of three day games during the preliminary rounds with a four-day final at Lord's. The big problem area was, of course, the possibility of drawn matches. Single-innings matches were dismissed as requiring two days and 'would lead to dull cricket and possibly irrational results'. Time limits with a decision on most runs per wicket were similarly rejected. The formula finally adopted takes a little believing but is true. In a drawn game, the winner would be the side which stood higher in the County Championship. Lest anyone should ever think of playing for a draw in the Cup because of a favourable position in the championship, the committee stated: 'County committees would be asked to direct their team to enter every match with the intention of winning.' Perhaps it is a sign of our cynical, over-professional times that makes this appear just a little naïve.

The proposals brought a very mixed reception, the arguments in *The Times* even carrying a religious flavour. The Archdeacon of Ipswich wrote deploring the idea because it would tend to encourage betting. C.B. Fry, now a senior citizen, rose immediately to defend his brainchild of forty-two years ago:

Dear Sir,
On the matter of Knock-out County cricket the feeling and opinion of the Archdeacon of Ipswich are entitled to great respect. But I would submit that his fear about the encourage-

ment of betting and pools is not necessary. Some experience first-hand of the game has fallen to my happy lot, and I have never heard a single bet made on a cricket match – not one. Of course, I may have been lucky. But I suggest that the Archdeacon would find it difficult to persuade any bookmaker to accept a bet on a cricket match or even quote odds. As for pools, surely, were they appropriate to any cricket, they would already have been exploited by the prosperous promoters? Cricket matches in all categories are just cricket matches.

C.B. Fry
Hamble.

Clerical support for Fry came from J. M. Swift (Diocesan House, Hove) and C. Booth (Farlington Rectory), but Mr H. Allen Job, the Secretary of the Church's Committee on Gambling, replied that in 1941 he had reported, 'Betting on cricket is not popular but bookmakers take bets freely on important matches. Cricket pools have gained considerable popularity in recent years. Three firms advertised twelve pools between them in 1938.'

In the end all of this debate was for nothing, for by June 1945 the ACCC had rejected the whole scheme for the 1946 season but promised to reconsider it once cricket routine had returned to normal. At the end of the 1946 season the idea was again rejected on the grounds of the unacceptable solution to the problem of drawn matches. Resurrected in 1955, on the one hundredth anniversary of the first proposed tournament, the answer was still 'no', with the provision, 'the counties will not lose sight of the idea'. The Altham committee recommended a trial tournament in 1957 but again the ACCC deferred the project due to the 'insurmountable difficulties'. Finally, of course, the ailing state of the county game in late 1961 almost mandated trying something new, and the long-standing problem of drawn matches was solved by the apparently simple solution of limited-overs, single-innings and one-day games.

The knock-out competition started in 1963, which turned out to be a significant year in the resurrection of cricket and was also a turning point in the life of the nation. In the political sphere Gaitskell died, Macmillan resigned and the Profumo affair erupted. At the same time the permissive sixties were beginning to get into full swing. In cricket the one-day novelty was played against the backdrop of a memorable Test series against the all-conquering West Indian team and there were no amateurs on display for the first time. Almost as if to signify that this marked the end of an era, two of the greatest names in cricket died that same year – Sir Jack Hobbs and Sir Pelham Warner. Frank Worrell duly took their place as a cricketing knight at the end of the season but his life was soon to be cut tragically short when his most valuable non-cricket work had only just begun.

The subsequent success of the Gillette Cup, as it was officially named in 1964, is well known. Also, the inauguration of other one-day competitions – the Players' Sunday League in 1969, the Benson and Hedges Cup in 1972, the Prudential Trophy in 1972, the Prudential World Cup in 1975 – has given cricket's finances new life. The one-day game also spread quickly in other countries, initially via sponsored domestic competitions. Australia started a knock-out cup in 1969/70, later to become the Gillette and subsequently McDonald's Cup, and others followed suit. Soon every touring team was also taking part in one-day internationals that have assumed almost the importance of Test Matches. Specialist limited-overs players are chosen for tours, though they are scarcely up to traditional Test Match standards.

It goes without saying that one-day cricket has become a dominating force in world cricket. The domination is financial – sponsors and television both covet these games above all else – but also the crowds indicate that a great many people prefer this type of cricket. While Test Matches have not yielded pride of place, ordinary county and state games surely have. As we have seen, this state of affairs owes its beginnings to the mood of the 1950s when the idea was first seriously mooted and when cricket seemed to be at one of its lowest points. The authorities were slow to take the hint but the prevailing social forces were not to be denied. When the break finally came, the trendy, swinging sixties were upon us and cricket joined the rest of the country in finally breaking free of post-war drabness.

The other innovative suggestion of the Ashton Committee – as if knock-out cups and the abolition of amateurs were not enough – concerned the institution of Sunday cricket. This was an old suggestion which had received much support from, among others, Cyril Washbrook in the early fifties. In 1956, however, the counties had overwhelmingly rejected the idea. By 1961 the mood for more organized Sunday leisure was underway and the Home Office asked all sporting bodies to submit their views on the subject; the counties, in concert with the changing public attitudes, provided a cautiously positive response. After several years of discussion and delay the first county championship games to include Sundays were played in 1965. Although this experiment was continued for two more years, the format of playing from 2:00 until 7:00 p.m. never really suited three-day cricket and in 1969 the Sunday League took over. This venture was fired by the enormous success of the Rothman's Cavaliers who had been playing televised Sunday games for charity and players' benefits. Greeted with tremendous enthusiasm at first, the Sunday league has certainly boosted finances and brought a new audience to view cricket matches. A certain lessening of interest is detectable lately – certainly the television coverage is significantly curtailed – and this is probably due to the sameness of so many of the games, even when they have close finishes. One cannot argue the fact, however, that in combination with the other developments outlined in this chapter, the one-day competitions certainly succeeded in making cricket 'brighter'. Whether they are desirable in every way will always remain a matter of personal taste.

5

All the Players are Gentlemen . . .

As we have already mentioned, exactly coincident with the introduction of one-day cricket came another revolutionary change that had been agonized over for years. On 26 November 1962, the Advisory Committee for County Cricket resolved that any distinction between amateurs and professionals should be abolished, and that henceforth all players should be known simply as 'cricketers'. 'Cricket To Break With Tradition!' read the newspaper headlines. The buildup to this momentous decision, described in this chapter, provides a fascinating example of the interplay between sport and the social development of the country at large.

Back at the turn of the century Albert Craig ('The Surrey Poet') would walk around The Oval reciting his famous dictum that 'All the Players are Gentlemen and all the Gentlemen are Players.' This simple phrase captures perfectly the feeling that prevailed for many years regarding the amateur and the professional in cricket. Their coexistence in first-class cricket was not only acceptable but highly desirable. There was a strong mutual respect between the two classifications. Their skills and contributions were significantly different yet uniquely complementary. For over 250 years the structure of the game had evolved in a slow and natural fashion and the basic distinction between 'Gentlemen' and 'Players' had never seriously been questioned. Attitudes towards this continuing status quo changed so rapidly during the 1950s, however, that the post-war development can justifiably be termed cricket's social revolution.

The dramatic erosion of the amateur's place in cricket, the reasons for which were both financial and social, is perhaps the most striking example of attitudes in cricket mirroring those of the society in which it is played. The working life of the first-class cricketer underwent changes just as profound and rapid as those occurring throughout all walks of life, and for the same reasons. We have noted earlier that after the deprivations and horrors of war there was a general feeling that a 'New Age' would evolve and this same desire fuelled many of the changes seen in cricket. Viewed in isolation, the decline of the amateur cricketer was a startling occurrence, but it holds no mystery when one considers the social backdrop against which it occurred.

In a country built on an established class system it was quite natural that cricket should develop its own equivalent. Throughout the eighteenth and early nineteenth centuries the 'grand' cricket matches were typically promoted by members of the gentry (the 'patrons' of cricket) who engaged men from the lower social strata to take part in the games. These players were typically farm workers, labourers and tradesmen and were often employed year-round on the estates of the patrons. Most of the Hambledon players were certainly professional cricketers, probably the first example of planned, professional team sport. In this way, a class distinction between the amateur and professional was taken for granted and built into cricket from its earliest days.

It was the emergence of the great touring sides, beginning with William Clarke's All-England Eleven in the mid-nineteenth century, that enabled professional cricketers to rise from this old master-servant relationship. The occupation of cricketer began to carry a certain prestige and remuneration superior to that of most agricultural or industrial labour. This trend continued through the early part of the twentieth century but by the 1950s we have seen that the financial aspects were becoming less attractive. In conjunction with the prevailing general social mood this encouraged the professional cricketer to become more sensitive to perceived injustices or inequalities with respect to his amateur colleagues.

The historical development of the amateur cricketer in parallel with the professional is also of interest. The amateur tradition really became most pronounced during the Victorian era when the Public Schools identified themselves with cricket and its character-building virtues. The excellent coaching and facilities at these schools naturally resulted in amateur players often being more stylish than professionals and many of the greatest batsmen in cricket's history appeared during the so-called Golden Age at the turn of the century. The unwritten law grew up that a public school background automatically made a player an amateur and so the sharp distinction was cemented into the fabric of the game. It should perhaps be emphasized that this was regarded as the natural order of things and was generally accepted by all parties as being in the best interests of the game. The professionals, just as much as the amateurs, would have been offended at any suggestion of integrating the two groups, so a mutually agreeable status quo existed for many years.

There were minor problems, of course. The touring elevens which saw the birth of the modern professional also brought into being the shamateur, most notably in the impressive shape of Dr W. G. Grace. As an example, while the professionals on the 1873/4 tour to Australia received £150 plus expenses, Grace himself was supposedly paid ten times that amount by the Melbourne Club. This suspicion of shamateurism which brought an official MCC definition of the amateur as early as 1878 (the year the first Australians toured as 'amateurs' and all received handsome payments) became even more pronounced in the Golden Age. It was a fine distinction whether the journalistic, advertising and coaching revenues of Fry, MacLaren and Jessop were somehow different to being paid for playing. Cricket, and their prowess at it, was their source of income whichever way one looks at it. W. W. Read and A. E. Stoddart were others whose status was open to question. Of course, one must respect the contemporary viewpoint on the definition of an amateur rather than apply present day logic. If cricket was not a player's main source of income it seems that the Victorian cricket world accepted him as an amateur. It was more a case of his 'attitude' and background than the purely financial side.

The word amateur derives from the Latin *amator*, or 'lover', implying that an amateur sportsman competes simply for the love of the game whereas the professional competes for money. The word was coined in 1788 to separate 'Gentleman Jack' Jackson, an aristocrat and boxer, from the professional bareknuckle fighters. Throughout the nineteenth century three categories of sportsman could be discerned: the professional, the amateur and the gentleman amateur. The last two were distinguished by whether or not the individual had to work for a living. In cricket of the Victorian and Edwardian eras both types of amateur existed, although the gentleman amateur has always been in very short supply.

The value and position of the amateur remained undisturbed right up to the Second World War. Thereafter, however, the financial and social forces of the times resulted in a distinct feeling of anachronism and the old pattern was challenged on many sides.

Cricket, being a game steeped in tradition, has always attracted many adherents from the more conservative sections of society. These people have often been ridiculed by the popular press and are typically referred to as the 'establishment'. Such generalizations can be dangerous. Certainly, the great majority of ex-Public School, MCC members who serve as cricket administrators are very far from the ludicrous, 'Colonel Blimp' figures that are so often depicted. There is no doubt that cricket has provided one of Britain's most sacrosanct homes for class consciousness, but mercifully this attitude has not been typical of those in administrative positions. This difference between the popular perception of those who run cricket and the actual facts is well demonstrated in the changes that occurred in the post-war period.

Professionals acquired a totally new acceptance in the early fifties, as far as the real establishment was concerned. In 1950 Leslie Ames, the former Kent and England wicket-keeper, was elected as the first professional on the Test Match selection committee (apart from Hobbs and Rhodes, who had been occasionally co-opted). In so doing he became the prototype for many who have followed and done worthy service such as Cyril Washbrook (1956) and more recently Ken Barrington and Alec Bedser.

Another example of the new acceptance, in line with the social changes evolving in the country at large, was the announcement, in 1948, that MCC would grant honorary life membership to a number of retired professional cricketers. This move was, in fact, instigated by G. O. Allen, a true member of cricket's establishment yet obviously a forward-looking thinker. This extension of MCC membership was not immediately granted to active players, however, and in 1951 we find the former Yorkshire and England amateur, Paul Gibb, agreeing to hold his MCC membership in suspension while he played as a professional for Essex. In fact, it was not until May 1955 that Len Hutton became the first professional elected an MCC cricket member while still playing county cricket.

In some cases the recognition of professional cricketers went considerably further than election to MCC; knighthoods were bestowed on the most prominent. Several ex-amateurs had previously been knighted for 'services to cricket' but these were mainly for administrative work such as that of F. E. Lacey, P. F. Warner, H. D. G. Leveson Gower and Frederick Toone. In 1949, however, Don Bradman became the first 'professional' cricketer so honoured. (Bradman was officially an amateur, and certainly had another job on the stock exchange, but he did earn a significant amount of money from cricket.) In the Coronation year, 1953, Jack Hobbs was added to the list, to be followed by Len Hutton in 1957 and Frank Worrell in 1963. In each case, of course, the individual was far more than simply a great cricket player. Each one had a major influence on his country and its relationship with the rest of the Commonwealth.

This new acceptance of professionals sometimes came as a surprise to those who had been schooled in the old traditions. When the 1950/1 MCC tourists visited South Australia the amateurs in the party were invited to accept honorary membership of the exclusive Adelaide Club, just as they had been since the earliest tours. The invitation was accepted but the press suggested that the professionals had been insulted. The MCC tour manager, Brigadier M. A. Green, has described how he had to explain to the mystified Club Secretary that 'the English cricket professional was now treated as an amateur in all ways socially'. Happily the professionals were subsequently included in the invitation in light of their 'altered social standing'.

There were other concessions made to the professional in these immediate post-war years; some were important while others were simply cosmetic. In 1946, at Lord's, the professionals began to use the same dressing-room and entrance to the field as the amateurs – a change which had begun during the wartime matches. This was a perfectly natural development of more enlightened times, although it may have owed something to the decreased number of amateurs playing county cricket in the forties and fifties. Tom Dollery, the Warwickshire and England batsman, has noted in his reminiscences how farcical it became for a solitary amateur to change in a dressing-room twice the size of the crowded professional accommodation. The degree of separation between amateurs and professionals varied quite a bit from county to county and ground to ground. Even before the war Brian Sellars (an amateur) used to lead his Yorkshire team through the professionals' gate whenever possible.

Another minor area in which an attempt was made to achieve equality between professionals and amateurs concerned the vexed question of initials. This apparently trivial topic surprisingly proved difficult to resolve. In 1941 the new editor of *The Times* had stated that, 'it was the duty of *The Times* to prepare for great social changes after the war'. True to its word, for the 1946 cricket season this most traditional of newspapers accorded all county cricketers, regardless of amateur or professional status, the honour of full initials before their names for the first time in its history. This was, according to the editor, 'entirely in consonance with the spirit of the age'. It may appear to be a minor development but to many of cricket's adherents it is just this type of minutiae of tradition and ritual which forms a great part of the game's charm. The fact that this apparently harmless gesture was of great significance to some is apparent in that it lasted for just one season. In May 1947, with none of the fanfare of the previous year, the likes of L. Hutton and D. C. S. Compton became plain Hutton and Compton again. The same gesture was simultaneously introduced on the 1946 scorecards at Lord's, again with the same subsequent reversal. The compromise method entailed having initials before the surnames for amateurs, and after the surname for professionals. This seems a clumsy way to distinguish between the two classifications but at least the pre-war title of Mr had long since disappeared.

One amusing sidelight to this whole affair of initials concerns Fred Titmus of Middlesex and England who was surprised during a match in the fifties to hear the public address announce as he walked out to bat: 'On your scorecards, F. J. Titmus should read Titmus, F. J.'

The more enlightened thinking towards professionals was not universally held, of course, and the more traditional approach can perhaps be characterized by the following letter which appeared in *The Times*, hopefully tongue-in-cheek, in 1950. The subject concerned initials and the modern tendency towards using a player's first name in the press and on radio:

> Dear Sir,
> How can Mr N. W. D. Yardley, who was so richly endowed by his godparents, maintain his moral authority as England's captain when the penny papers either 'Norman' him or write him down in the score sheet as mere 'N. Yardley'? Meanwhile, his team-mate, 'Wardle', is allotted a wholly superfluous initial 'J'.
>
> J. C. H. Hadfield
> The Savile Club

Despite these isolated examples of outdated thinking, all the evidence points to a rapid post-war reduction in the degree of differentiation between professionals and amateurs. One player who was well qualified to comment on this change was Tom Dollery, whose career fell on both sides of the war and who was an early professional county captain. He referred to: 'the years of discrimination which lasted in its most acute form right up to 1939'. This sharp pre- and post-war contrast was also in the mind of Brian Statham when he wrote: 'I would not have enjoyed the days when there was a sharp division between the paid and the unpaid. The professional had little status.' Bill Edrich has written that, 'There was an austerity about Lord's in 1934, highlighted by the great chasm in status between the amateurs and the professionals.' While these quotes illustrate a change in atmosphere after the war, one cannot accept that many professionals harboured very strong grudges about their amateur colleagues.

This sensible and natural mellowing of cricket's class distinction could well have resulted in the continuing existence of amateurs in professional cricket, as many would have desired. Ideally, the amateur brought a spirit and a style which is often absent from the professional and which is deeply mourned. The major reason that the amateur was doomed, however, proved to be financial. The dominant driving force for removing amateurs was surely based on the perceived unfairness of shamateurism. If England's leading amateurs had not been forced by the facts of modern economic life to derive income, directly or indirectly, from their cricket prowess, then there would have been no pressing reason to simply eliminate the title of 'amateur'. The argument is somewhat circular, however, for as soon as the leading amateurs became shamateurs their essential difference from professionals was already gone. The independent attitude of the true amateur virtually disappeared with the war, and ninety-nine percent of county cricketers were 'professional' in the most important sense, namely attitude, long before 1962. The legislation of that year was simply a belated, de facto recognition of something which had already occurred. The modern amateurs such as Bailey, Cowdrey and May were full-time cricketers who displayed all the grim determination of their professional colleagues. They experienced the same pressures and were far removed from the old-style amateur who would play in perhaps half his county's matches, walking in and out of the team as his business or teaching commitments allowed. A few maintained this tradition in the fifties but they were a dying breed.

With this increased awareness or assumption of shamateurism there came a steady erosion of the prestige formerly associated with amateurs. With the increased number of Tests the Gentlemen versus Players match was no longer regarded as a centrepiece of the cricket season except among the older traditionalists. Each year brought increasing calls for the abolition of the fixture which one newspaper called, 'otiose and obsolete'. Also, the very term 'Gentlemen' for the amateurs was considered by the more sensitive as a subtle sneer at the professional and recalled the old master-servant relationship. Not that the players seemed to object – the criticisms usually came from people far removed from the game itself. In common with this, the traditional amateur cricket events – University and Public School matches – dramatically lost their appeal. In the late forties these games had still maintained their traditional public attention. With paper in short supply the *Cricketer* magazine saved space by eliminating full scores of all county games except the University ones – the very opposite of what has happened in recent years. The Eton versus Harrow game was still a highlight of the social calendar. In 1947 the newly engaged Princess Elizabeth and Philip Mountbatten accompanied the King and Queen to the game and were the centre of attention for the throngs of débutantes in their fashionable 'New Look'. In contrast, by 1963 the Public School matches attracted little attention and the universities' continued participation as first-class sides was openly debated; their fixtures were, at best, enjoyable practice for county second XI players.

This declining prestige of the amateur was further fuelled by repeated sniping, not only in the popular press but also in the reminiscences and articles written by (or ghosted for) professional cricketers. Some made the simple and understandable argument that a fellow professional should not lose his place in the team to an amateur whose pleasure was therefore jeopardizing someone's livelihood. Brian Statham expressed this as follows:

> Of course there is jealousy between these two classes. It's only human nature. Most professionals dislike seeing part-timers taking the places of men who get their living from the game.

Others hit more strongly at this basic feeling of 'them' and 'us'. Dollery wrote in 1952 that he would not wish his son to become a professional because of this feeling of being 'faintly inferior, a person who is "not quite" '. It was this feeling of inferiority, according to Dollery, which led to the 'freemasonry' among professionals and the pride taken in craftsmanship and integrity. Frank Tyson, a deep thinking and intelligent cricketer, was particularly militant on the subject, writing that an amateur was, 'a cricketer, shrewd at heart, who from ultraistic sooner than altruistic motives, is ashamed or unwilling to admit that he earns his coppers from the game. In the final count, he still makes his living out of the game.' Other statements in his autobiography, *A Typhoon Called Tyson*, included 'The amateur-professional apartheid does nothing but harm to any team and particularly to a touring side . . . The pretended and superficial classification into paid and unpaid players ought not to exist in the man-to-man relationship of cricket.'

One wonders how much this type of thing was simply designed to sell books, but, even if it was not a fair reflection of the opinions of most cricketers, it is of interest that there was a receptive audience amongst cricket's public for such statements. By the early sixties, the popular press had almost turned the amateur/professional question into a crusade along the lines of 'equality for the workers'. While this was going on, however, it is hard to believe that Tyson and other professionals allowed such critical thoughts to intrude into their everyday relationships with amateur colleagues. Denis Compton, whose career spanned both sides of the war, was probably pretty near the mark when he wrote:

> When I began to play there was quite a marked distinction between the amateur and the professional; a sort of gulf or distance between them, placed there by a tradition which may have tended to be snobbish, but so far as I could judge, it never really affected the relationship, person to person, of the amateur and the professional players concerned. I never minded or felt the distinction, and I don't remember any of the other professionals minding either.

Doug Insole, the Essex captain of the fifties, has commented along similar lines:

> If any snobbery exists, it is outside the game and not among the players themselves. In days when amateurs and professionals share the same amenities, the same hotels – and very often the same bat and pads – it is not easy to understand how in former times there was so much segregation. First-class cricket has moved with the times to the extent that, in my

experience, there has been no occasion on which any sort of unrest or discontent brought about by difference of status has existed in a team of which I have been a member.

Another important indication of the changing position of the amateur was the increasing tendency for ex-public schoolboys to adopt cricket as a profession. In conjunction with the spread of shamateurism, this further reduced the differential between amateur and professional to one of name only. In the early nineteenth century, careers for public school and university men were more or less limited to the Army, the Church and the Law. By the turn of the century it had become quite normal to become a merchant, doctor, author or artist. After the Second World War in England, however, almost any career was acceptable, including banking, television, science, engineering and county cricketer.

In the years before the Second World War there had been the occasional example of a public schoolboy becoming a professional, often in unusual circumstances. E. J. Diver, of Surrey and Warwickshire, who represented both the Gentlemen and the Players, has been claimed to be the first such example but, in fact, Pease School was not a Public School when he attended it. The earliest actual cases were probably those of R. F. Vibart and Reginald Wood, both of whom fell from grace after starting their lives as 'gentlemen'. Wood was at Charterhouse where he appeared in the XI in 1876. A decade later he had emigrated to Australia, played some local cricket and been called into a Test Match by the injury-stricken English touring side. His life in Australia was subsequently unsuccessful, however, and he later became a professional to at least two clubs before dying as a lowly book-keeper in New South Wales.

Vibart provided a similar unhappy tale. In the Harrow XI from 1893-96, he was a good all-round sportsman being in the football XI as well as the Public Schools' boxing champion. Although he went up to Cambridge in 1896 his stay there was cut short and he embarked on a mysterious spell in South America. This obviously brought no business success for, on his return, Vibart was forced to make a living as professional to a number of schools and clubs in the West Country and even played county cricket for Cornwall. After the war, in which he served in the Public School Battalion, his life included various court appearances and drunken brawls before he finally took his own life in 1934.

These stories of Vibart and Wood are interesting but they hardly indicate that cricket was considered as a proper profession for ex-Harrovians and Carthusians. In the 1890s, however, three public schoolboys did appear as professional cricketers, apparently without any of these unusual circumstances. These were C. J. B. Wood (Northants and Leicestershire), G. J. Thompson (Northants) and C. P. Buckenham (Essex). The two latter players had distinguished cricket careers, appearing occasionally for England, and were the first two genuine examples of 'gentlemen' professionals. Wood, a Wellingborough boy, played a few games for Northants as a professional before joining the Leicestershire groundstaff in 1896. After continuing to appear as a professional for a short time he was finally offered the post of assistant treasurer and automatically became an amateur, going on to an illustrious career as captain of the XI from 1914-20.

Throughout the twentieth century there continued to be the odd case of professional ex-public schoolboys, but generally a way could be found to pay such cricketers without publicly acknowledging the fact. After the war, however, a steadily increasing number of young men were clearly not worried about maintaining the pretence of being called amateurs. We have seen how Paul Gibb became the first 'old blue' to play professional cricket (for Essex, after playing as an amateur for his native Yorkshire) and he was followed by other Cambridge players in Goonesena and Parsons. Also in the Essex team Roy Ralph took the honest decision of turning professional when he could no longer afford to play as an amateur. The social climate had clearly changed dramatically, and the career choice of subsequent England internationals such as M. J. Stewart, P. J. Sharpe, J. D. F. Larter, D. W. and P. E. Richardson, and G. Millman hardly raised an eyebrow. These all occurred during the fifties in the aftermath of Hutton's landmark appointment as England captain. There were many others, like N. I. Thomson, D. C. Morgan and R. A. Gale, who enjoyed long and successful county careers. The profession of cricketer, which had for a long time been respectable but limited to State schoolboys and non-graduates, was now open to men from any section of society.

One of the public schoolboys who turned professional in the early 1950s was Mickey Stewart of Surrey. Now the cricket manager for the county, he has contributed the following thoughts on the subject for this chapter:

The amateur and professional situation had been a traditional part of the English first class cricket season for many, many years. In the 50s it was very apparent that 'gentlemen of leisure' were becoming fewer and fewer and therefore the time that a person could spend away from his particular job in order to play cricket as an amateur was becoming more limited. It was a time of social change as well and the social life of the professional was becoming closer and closer to that of the amateur, whereas they had been poles apart in previous decades.

A certain amount of shamateurism had always existed in the game but at the same time there were plenty of genuine amateurs who provided a great number of plus points.

When I myself turned professional in 1953 after completing National Service, it was considered unusual, my having been educated at a public school. I remember at the time the name of G. S. Watson of Leicestershire, another public schoolboy in the 30s who had turned professional, being quoted. However, many young players from similar backgrounds took the professional route in the late 50s early 60s and I think it is a fact that in the present day a figure of around 40% of professional cricketers are products of public and leading grammar schools.

It was quite a decision when I myself turned professional, not so much as far as I was concerned, but I had many people advising me to take the amateur route into the game. Apart from realizing my ambition of becoming a professional, I remember that a main point I considered at the time was that I was aware that not all amateurs became established in a county side on merit and I always wanted to be sure in my mind that my playing performance earned my place.

The amateur and professional situation in English first class cricket had always been a strange one and was never really understood by cricketers from other countries. Amateurs changing in different dressing rooms from professionals and going out of different gates in spite of all being members of the same side is difficult to understand. As the first professional captain of Surrey, I was asked by the Cricket Committee to change in the original amateurs' dressing-room. For a few weeks I reluctantly did so, but it was foreign to my own personality and I was soon back in my own spot in the professional dressing-room and changed there for the next ten years whilst I was captain of the county side.

The gentlemen and players situation was really just an extension of part of the social life of the country in general and now on the surface does not exist, similar to the many changes of the general social life in England today.

George Watson, incidentally, played as an amateur for Kent and then turned professional for Leicestershire. Stewart was probably compared to him because they both played football for Corinthian Casuals and Charlton Athletic.

With this background in mind the step of calling all players 'cricketers' was the most natural development in the world. By the early sixties the actual difference between amateur and professional was hard to see and its continuation was at times almost farcical. The Richardson brothers, Peter and Derek, were from the same family and the same school. They played in the same county side, Worcestershire, and appeared together for England yet one was a professional (Derek) and one an amateur (Peter). To cap it all, when Peter joined Kent as a professional in 1959, Worcestershire tried everything to keep him and even announced that Richardson 'was made aware that he would suffer no financial loss by remaining with Worcestershire as an amateur'.

The decline of the amateur can also be charted in a purely numerical sense (Figure 1). Here, the percentage of amateurs among county cricketers (championship matches only) is plotted between the years 1890 and 1962. The number was fairly stable in the range 40-50% from most of those years but the dip after 1946 is truly dramatic. Each year saw fewer and fewer amateurs, even including those who only played one or two games per season, and by the early sixties the ratio was barely one amateur to every eight professionals.

Strangely enough this apparent decline of the traditional amateur coincided with the emergence of a series of marvellous batsmen from the university sides of the forties and fifties. In the early post-war years John Dewes and Hubert Doggart broke a host of batting records at Cambridge and appeared to have the cricketing world at their feet. They were amateurs of the old style, however, in that they could only spare time for the game as their schoolteaching duties allowed. During the Golden Age, a MacLaren or a Jackson could continue an England career despite this handicap, but it was just no longer possible in the professional world of the post-war era. The Rev. David Sheppard was another amateur who was essentially lost to cricket because of a conflict with his other profession. Two of the classic university batsmen, Peter May and Colin Cowdrey, were somewhat different, however, in that they became full-time Test and county cricketers; Ted Dexter later followed in their footsteps. It is interesting that Dewes, Doggart, Sheppard, May and John Warr all played for England around 1950 while still undergraduates. In the entire pre-war history of Test cricket only ten other students had been so honoured and since that time only Derek Pringle has joined the select list. On the whole though, these dazzling players were only isolated examples very much against the trend of declining influence by quality amateur players.

The other key feature in the changing social position of professional cricketers concerns the question of team captaincy. Here again we find revolutionary changes occurring in the very shortest of time spans.

The post-war rise of professional captaincy began in the first

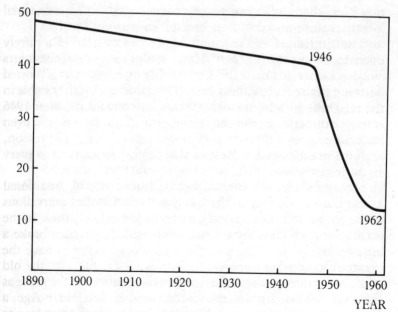

Figure 1.   Decline of the Amateur – County Championship Matches 1890-1962

season, 1946, when Leslie Berry was appointed captain of Leicestershire in the absence of any available amateurs. There had been professional county captains before and, in fact, Berry was the second to captain Leicestershire (Ewart Astill had one highly successful season in 1935). One of the finest players ever to appear for the county, Berry led the side for the first three post-war years with success and skill, but in 1949 when he was still batting up to his best standard, he was superseded by an amateur, Major S. J. Symington. Symington only played eighteen games in 1949 and the following year returned to his full-time Army career. At this distance in time it seems that Berry's demotion was premature without a worthy successor, but the three years he was in office were important in the development of the professional captain.

In 1948, Berry was joined by another professional county captain, H. E. 'Tom' Dollery of Warwickshire. Like Berry, Dollery had been the team's senior professional with an outstanding pre-war career behind him and was still at his peak as a batsman. Also like Berry, he became captain by default when there was no amateur available. When it became apparent, however, that Dollery was an excellent captain in his own right, Warwickshire asked him to become an amateur but he refused and continued to lead the county until retirement in 1955. He was even more successful than Berry, leading an average-strength Warwickshire team to the County Championship in 1951 and winning praise from almost everybody associated with the county game. Dollery, who incidentally had attended a public school, more than anyone else made the post of professional captain acceptable.

This practice of a professional becoming an amateur in order to captain his county had occurred several times, most notably in the case of Wally Hammond. Fred Titmus wrote of this: 'Many county sides still cling to the idea that it is not in the nature of the professional to make a good captain unless, of course, he turns amateur, in which case his basic nature undergoes radical change apparently.'

In 1950 another important step was taken with the appointment of James Langridge to captain Sussex. This change, however, was far from a smooth transition. When Hugh Bartlett resigned the captaincy in February he was originally replaced by Hubert Doggart and R. G. Hunt in a shared arrangement. Before the season started, however, there was a vote of no confidence in the committee, which resigned en masse. After some considerable fuss, Langridge was appointed as caretaker captain, a post he held successfully for three years.

Berry, Dollery and Langridge all carried out their captaincy so capably that most of the old objections were soon discounted. The popular beliefs that a professional would not be able to exert discipline over fellow-professionals, would be hesitant to drop them from the team, that he could not be independent of the committee and that he would be too defensive, were shown to be unfounded. The Rev. David Sheppard, who was forever being championed as the right 'sort' for captaincy, had this to say:

> It was felt that an amateur can more easily snap his fingers at the committee, when that is a good thing to do, than someone who is a 'servant of the club'. Yet I can think of an amateur county captain who was the complete slave of his committee and of professional captains who have had a most independent spirit. The personality of the man himself rather than his status is what counts. And if we start thinking about status, the men who we should consider first are those who are the backbone of the first-class game – the professional cricketers.

The same attitude has been expressed by Geoff Edrich, who played under amateur and professional captains for Lancashire:

> I don't think there was any change of spirit in a team when professional captains were introduced. I feel it all depended on what type of person the skipper was, whether he be pro or amateur.

Anyway, the move for more professional captains was relentlessly gaining momentum, fuelled by the fact that there were so few good amateurs available. In 1951, Denis Compton was made joint captain of Middlesex with Bill Edrich (formerly a professional but now amateur) but it was in 1952 that the most significant single event occurred in the emancipation of the professional cricketer – Len Hutton was appointed captain of England for the series against India.

The playing success which Hutton brought to the England captaincy is now well known. His reign was not without its troubles and controversies, however, and it took a heavy personal toll on Hutton himself, the pressure probably foreshortening his career by a number of years. Nevertheless, the character, skill and bearing which he brought to the job finally put an end to the amateur monopoly of captaincy. The original decision to appoint Hutton was a brave one, typical, let it be emphasized again, of the progressive thinking characteristic of Lord's during this period. There was a tremendous surge of press and public comment, both for and against, which must have made the pressures enormous. Bill Edrich has perfectly summarized the situation: 'Hutton's appointment was only grudgingly received by those who failed to understand the social revolution that was unfolding.' After his first overseas tour as captain, to the West Indies in 1953/1954, there was a considerable lobby for his replacement by the Rev. David Sheppard. After this troublesome tour, full of incidents and accusations of time-wasting, defensiveness and poor player behaviour, it would have been very easy to make such a change. Before the crucial 1954/1955 tour to Australia Hutton's detractors could point to his recent injuries and apparent loss of batting form. The selectors, however, were determined to stick to Hutton (although only by a one-vote majority), thereby providing the most striking example that the days of 'old school tie' selections were over and had no place in the modern game of cricket. As we have already discussed, Hutton has often been criticized for popularizing the most insidious modern problem in the game, the slow over-rate. He has also been accused of introducing a distinct coolness between the English and Australian teams of his day. Although he may have been less openly friendly to the opposition than Norman Yardley, his coolness could hardly compare with that of the pre-war Douglas Jardine. It was rumoured, however, that the controversial decision to drop Alec Bedser during the 1954/1955 tour owed as much to his refusal to stop fraternizing with the opposition as to his bowling skills. Hutton may have been, as Colin Cowdrey said, 'full of contradictions with a streak of isolationism', but he was without doubt a pivotal figure in developing the social balance of post-war cricket.

After the first tentative appointments of Berry, Dollery and Langridge, Hutton's staggering success in Test matches was finally instrumental in opening the floodgates as far as professional county captains were concerned. By 1956 Jack Crapp, George Emmett (both Gloucestershire), Doug Wright (Kent), Cyril Washbrook (Lancashire), Dennis Brookes (Northamptonshire), Reg Perks (Worcestershire), Maurice Tremlett (Somerset) and Eric Hollies (Warwickshire) had all taken over the leadership of their counties from amateur colleagues. In some cases the county committees acted with almost unseemly haste. W. Murray-Wood was the amateur captain of Kent in 1952 and 1953. In July of his second year, however, the committee asked him to resign to make way for another man, which he refused to do. On 6 August the committee met to discuss the issue and were informed that certain senior members of the side were reluctant to continue playing under Murray-Wood. The very next day after this early demonstration of 'player power', the club announced, during Canterbury Week, that Murray-Wood was to be superseded by a professional, England bowler Doug Wright, for the rest of the season. It was made clear that Murray-Wood had been sacked after refusing to resign.

Another aspect of this type of pressure from professionals concerned Billy Sutcliffe who, when he took over the captaincy from Norman Yardley, received very little help or encouragement from the senior Yorkshire players. Instead of trying to make a difficult job easier they apparently went as far as to petition for his removal. In a similar circumstance, Nigel Howard at Lancashire was left alone by the senior players so that he could 'Make a mess of it'. Instead, he became a very good captain and moulded a successful team.

After this early rush to go along with the new trend, things settled down and in the years between 1954 and 1962 there were never less than four professional county captains in any season and never more than six. A few counties kept to traditional appointments and some never had a professional captain right up to 1962, the year that amateurs ceased to be recognized. Yorkshire, in the true tradition of Lord Hawke, resisted for some time but finally in 1960 they chose Vic Wilson to be their first professional captain this century. Even Leonard Hutton had been unable to win this coveted post, except in Yardley's absence.

Despite this sudden influx of professional captains it is probably fair to say that apart from Hutton and Dollery none of those appointed in the fifties became truly outstanding captains. The leading county captains of the period were probably Surridge, Wooller, M. J. K. Smith, May, Insole, Brown, Ingleby-Mackenzie and a few others, all amateurs. In fact, towards the end of the period there were distinct signs of a return to the old method of choosing an amateur with little or no first-class experience. Between the years 1958 and 1962 C. T. M. Pugh (Gloucestershire), J. F. Blacklidge (Lancashire), J. R. Burnet (Yorkshire), P. I. Bedford (Middlesex) and D. Kirby (Leicestershire) all fell into this category. With the exception of Burnet, none of these were wildly successful and the practice, which was not really in harmony with the modern game, virtually disappeared after 1962.

What of the attitudes of the individuals concerned with first-class cricket? While it is dangerous to generalize, some trends during the years leading up to 1962 do emerge. The post-war professional cricketer, as we have seen, expected and received greater equality in terms of treatment, captaincy and general recognition. The one area of dissatisfaction concerned shamateurism. In this context we have quoted passages from Frank Tyson's autobiography. Referring to these more recently, he stated:

> My criticism of the amateur arose from my background, which educated me to believe that every man should earn his living from what he was doing and doing well – not from what he pretended to do, just to maintain social face. It did not help to hear some amateurs say they could not afford to turn professional.

Another professional stated: 'There was a feeling that the amateur system was outdated. There were quite a number of so-called amateurs making money through cricket anyway.' In 1962 Ted Dexter freely admitted that he made a good deal more from cricket than from business. Robin Marler announced in 1958 that 'few amateurs have played for England since 1953 without becoming involved in financial gain'. Bill Alley has told the story – possibly apocryphal – of how he was offered terms by Nottinghamshire before ultimately joining Somerset. One of the leading amateurs is supposed to have said, 'Let's get things straight now. If you come to Notts, you won't be the top money man. I shall be getting more money than you.'

These feelings certainly did not lead to open resentment between professionals and amateurs; in fact, the pointlessness of the façade was openly recognized by many amateurs. Dollery again:

> It would not be true to say that professionals have been embittered . . . the companionship of the cricket field has prevented that, with the knowledge that many amateurs disliked the use of separate dressing-rooms and separate gates even more than we did. But it would not have been in human nature to have been unaffected by it.

What of cricket's administrators, the so-called establishment? The first official move in recognition of the post-war social changes was the setting up of a special MCC committee in the winter of 1957/1958. Under the chairmanship of the Duke of Norfolk, and composed exclusively of former and current amateur players, the committee was charged with examining the whole question of amateur status. Their brief was very much to find ways of preserving amateurism while attempting to eliminate 'anomalies'.

While *The Times* correspondent stated, that 'no one doubts that the days of amateurism in the cold letter of the law are past', the result of the inquiry was something of a whitewash. It was concluded that the 'distinctive status of the amateur cricketer was not obsolete, was of great value to the game and should be preserved'. Professionals, the committee reported, support this view but were opposed to the 'anomalies' – by which was meant shamateurism. Only two committee members, of whom the Rev. David Sheppard tells us he was one, dissented from the published recommendations. The contentious issue of broken-time payments was discussed, and it was recommended that amateurs on MCC tours should be reimbursed for loss of earnings while out of the country. The committee did concede, however, that the custom of awarding amateurs double the expense allowance of professionals on tours was illogical. It was further ruled that the receipt of fees for advertising, writing or broadcasting on cricket was not inconsistent with amateur status. This softening of the official interpretation of amateurism also embraced the full-time cricket administrator who was reassured of his amateur ranking. It was not stated exactly how a 'full-time' county secretary like Wilfred Wooller (Glamorgan) or Trevor Bailey (Essex) could be available to play regular first-class cricket. Although both of these individuals worked tirelessly for their counties it is doubtful whether their full remuneration was for the secretarial duties. Certainly, when Wooller announced his retirement as a player Glamorgan refused his offer to stay on as secretary at the same salary – instead offering him a lower sum.

Clearly, around this time the official view was still one of turning a blind eye towards shamateurism and trying to find artificial ways of encouraging amateurs. Against the economic facts of post-war life this attitude was certainly doomed to failure. In the eyes of some people, however, no price was too great to pay including, if necessary, the destruction of traditional first-class cricket in England. For this is effectively what was suggested several times by the Secretary of the MCC, R. Aird, as well as by a number of other influential people. The proposed scheme, and it has surfaced in various forms since, involved only playing cricket at weekends. This would have had the effect of putting the vast majority of professionals out of work and would have drastically reduced county memberships, all for the sake of helping so-called amateurs to play county cricket. The counties were more realistic, however, and have always resisted anything that would reduce membership. The real solution to encouraging more university graduates into cricket has since been found to be the very simple one of higher salaries, which in turn have been provided by sponsorship. It is interesting to note that as long ago as 1908 Sir Home Gordon was advocating a restructuring of county cricket to enable more amateurs to play. 'That is the crying need of contemporary cricket,' he wrote, adding 'The modern professional is a fine type of man, but the pseudo-amateur who plays the game for what he can make out of it is a craft sailing under false colours. When an amateur's "expenses" are returned at a sum double the professional's fee, and when amateurs' washing bills are paid, these things become a drag on the sportsmanship of cricket.'

The Norfolk committee's decisions, of course, merely delayed the inevitable, and by February 1962 the whole tone of the discussion had changed radically. The Ashton committee (originally chaired by Colonel R. S. Rait Kerr) which had already been responsible for the introduction of the knock-out competition (later to become the Gillette Cup), discussed the issue and were within one vote of recommending the abolition of amateurs. This about-face was passed on to the ACCC who discussed it at length in March without voting. In November, however, the narrow Ashton vote against abolition was reversed by a clear majority, the resolution for all players to be 'cricketers' being proposed by Glamorgan. The decision had finally been made and was generally received very favourably.

To summarize this phase in cricket development, the attitude of post-war cricket administrators tended to be progressive with regard to upgrading the professional status, but was for a long time obsessed with preserving the 'amateur contributions of leadership and adventurous spirit'. By 1962 it was clear that these qualities were as likely to be found in a professional as an amateur and the 'establishment' was generally happy to give way to the inevitable. Even in this year, however, one was able to read in the new edition of Altham and Swanton's *History of Cricket* criticism of the fact that increasing numbers of grammar schoolboys were winning blues at Oxford and Cambridge. These unfortunates were accused of 'crowding out' public-school cricketers who therefore 'never know the early summer glories of Fenners and the Parks'. This trend was 'restricting the flow of natural leaders to the game'. E. W. Swanton, who wrote this passage, probably did not mean to appear critical of grammar schoolboys since he is on record many times as a genuine supporter of cricketers whatever their school background. He is a shrewd and moderate progressive in his thinking about the game but, nevertheless, these quotes do embody some of what John Arlott has described as 'the woolly romanticism and anachronistic feudalism' so long associated with English cricket. During the last twenty years the game has definitely moved towards a more classless atmosphere, in common, of course, with so many other walks of British life.

When cricket is compared with other sports the administrators and committee men again emerge in a favourably progressive light. Cricket had always been different to rugby, athletics and tennis in which amateurs and professionals were not allowed to compete together in the same game or tournaments. The November 1962 decision made cricket, with table tennis, the only major sport without recognized amateurs. Lawn tennis had been deliberating for three years about whether to make Wimbledon an open tournament and was to carry on agonizing until 1968. Soccer put off the inevitable until the late seventies by which time payments to nonleaguers had made a mockery of the traditional amateur game. Athletics and rugby union are still subject to unpleasant rows and scandals over the issue. Cricket has had enough arguments recently and we can only be thankful that shamateurism has not had to be one of them.

6
Bringing the Game Into Disrepute

Cricket, like many other human activities, has thrown up its fair share of arguments and controversies over the years. In the early Hambledon era it might have been caused by the addition of a third stump or the width of the bat. In the nineteenth century it started with accusations of deliberately losing games to win bets, and continued through the heated debates for roundarm, and later overarm, bowling. Before the First World War, Australian cricket underwent the upheaval caused by the clash between leading players and the newly formed Board of Control. The result was a tour of England with six of the finest players, including Trumper, Hill and Armstrong, staying behind in Australia. These controversies have been occasionally violent, as witness the famous incident in which Clem Hill's fist connected with Peter McAlister's jaw. Perhaps the most acrimonious of all was the Bodyline crisis of 1932/3 when governments were involved and future Anglo-Australian cricket relations were in serious jeopardy.

Despite this long tradition of argument and strife, it seems that the immediate post-war era saw world cricket, and particularly English cricket, subjected to an unusually frequent series of incidents which familiarized the phrase 'bringing the game into disrepute'. Perhaps it was the increasing glare of modern publicity and the trend for media sensation that turned disagreements into 'rows' and 'affairs' which filled the newspaper columns with monotonous regularity. We had the 'Wardle Affair', the 'Laker Row', the 'Graveney Incident', the 'Throwing Affair' and many others which will be discussed in this chapter. These incidents were not confined to the fifties, either, since they paved the way for such later newspaper delights as the 'D'Oliveira Affair', the 'Close Sacking', the 'Packer Affair', the 'South African Rebel Tour' and the 'Boycott Case'. These incidents no longer occasionally bring the game into disrepute – they form an ever-present part of the modern game.

If there was a common thread running through the post-war controversies it was that many involved some sort of confrontation between players and administrators. Viewed in this light, the incidents become of great interest to a social history of the game. The two groups disagreed over certain issues, as they had always done, but in the new social climate which demanded equality, players would not bow down to authority. Intransigent positions were taken, harsh words were spoken and the old principle of keeping the argument away from the public went out of the window. The popular press, usually on the side of the player, often became the debating ground and this led to more antagonism. Some have attempted to correlate the player versus administrator theme as being akin to employee versus employer, worker against management, even lower class versus upper class – the comparisons are tempting to make but perhaps should not be taken too far. Nonetheless, there is no doubt that many of the cricketing confrontations were simply another manifestation of the social forces at work throughout every walk of life. Since the war there has been an increasing tendency towards militant industrial action. In 1957 more days were lost to strikes than in any year since 1926, the year of the General Strike. This increasing tendency for demanding one's rights certainly spilled over into cricket. In that same year of 1957, Tony Lock wrote: 'If a union is not practicable, then prospects of forming a Professional Cricketers' Association on the same lines as the Professional Golfers' Association are worthy of investigation.' In fact, the formation of a Cricketers' Association was delayed until 1968 when the present highly successful and non-militant organization was formed, but the desire for some sort of voice in the organization of the game was clearly felt in the late fifties. Around this time there also appears to have been some sort of reaction from Lord's. Colin Cowdrey has described, in his autobiography, the disastrous 1958/9 tour to Australia in which England lost the Ashes 4-0 amid argument and acrimony over a host of things, particularly the throwing issue. Cowdrey states:

In the inquest which followed that calamitous tour there seemed to emerge a line of thought which was to have a profound effect upon English cricket for the next decade. It was held to be high time that the players were brought down to size. Our defeat in Australia was explained away by an excess of player power. In future there should be less room for personality cult and a tighter enforcement of discipline.

As with many of cricket's social issues, such as the amateur/ professional question, it would be foolish to picture all the cricketers of the day spending their time pondering the desire for so-called 'player power' or confrontation with authority. Nevertheless, it should still be valid to rationalize the various controversies in terms of this overall atmosphere of the fifties which demanded equality and rejected suppression.

The earliest post-war cricket controversies erupted in Australia where the always strained relations between many of the players and the Board of Control seemed to deteriorate even further. There had been a long tradition of the Australian Board being somewhat remote from and even antagonistic towards the players, dating from the Great Australian Row of 1912. Since that time, any player with a touch of precociousness or free spirit has felt the wrath of the Board sooner or later. In Australia's case the authorities of that time were not only of a different generation to the players but, more significantly, they had never played cricket at a high level themselves. This situation has changed considerably in recent times but for many years there was a yawning gap between the players and the Board. The notable exception to these non-player administrators during the forties and fifties was, of course, Sir Donald Bradman, whose word was virtually law for a great many years. Here the historian runs into a slight problem as it is impossible for anyone remote from the inner circles of Australian cricket to give a valid assessment of Bradman's role. It is easy to find a number of people who will criticize Bradman and accuse him of being responsible for any number of behind the scenes intrigues. One only has to read the books of Jack Fingleton, Dick Whitington and Keith Miller to get more than a hint that many of Bradman's fellow-players did not exactly warm to him. English players noticed this too, and Denis Compton summarized: 'Bradman, to put it mildly, had some qualities which were difficult to admire. One never had the impression he forgave easily.' To be fair, the glowing written tributes to Bradman far outweigh the criticisms, although the former have often come from non-playing colleagues.

Apart from the fact that Bradman was a hard man, off the field as well as on it, and therefore was not given to the easy-going banter and camaraderie of the dressing-room, especially before the war, certain specific accusations have been made. These nearly all involve non-selections for tours and include the pre-war exclusion of Clarrie Grimmett from the 1938 tour to England, and the omissions of Cecil Pepper (1945/6 to New Zealand) and Keith Miller (1949/50 to South Africa). These decisions have repeatedly been put down to some sort of revenge for slights or insults which Bradman had supposedly received from the players in question. We shall never know the rights and wrongs of the issues but, as Godfrey Evans put it: 'The Don was not a man to be trifled with.'

In a way these incidents are not strictly relevant to the theme of post-war player suppression in Australia and are more personal in nature. They were not principally a result of Board attitudes – in fact, during his playing career Bradman was probably as much at loggerheads with the Board as most other players. After he retired, however, he became the game's most influential administrator and ran straight into one of Australia's most infamous controversies – the Sidney Barnes affair. This episode clearly demonstrated the Board's sensitivity to even the slightest criticism by players.

Barnes, on statistical evidence one of the finest batsmen ever to represent Australia, was an enigma amongst modern players – a gloriously unpredictable and fascinating character. Like his famous English namesake, Sid Barnes had a realistically high regard for his own ability and was not bashful about telling others. Well-liked by his team-mates and closest friends he was anathema to the administrators and controllers of cricket in Australia. Ray Robinson, the doyen of Australian cricket writers, described Barnes perfectly in a short essay so appropriately titled 'The Artful Dodger'. He wrote:

> Those who know how to take his assertiveness and banter like him. They find him without humbug, grasping yet generous, hard as nails yet quickly sympathetic . . . in all the criticism of Barnes for flagrant showmanship and cross-grained behaviour, the most severe comments come from those who know him from afar, the least from the cricketers who have played with and against him.

Here then was the perfect recipe for conflict – a highly individual, brash, opportunistic showman against a group of staid elder statesmen with a reputation for keeping the players in their place. From his first tour in 1938 to the effective end of his career in 1951 Barnes had been in many minor scrapes and misunderstandings with the Board and occasionally with Bradman. Barnes was probably the only player Bradman ever batted with who attempted to match The Don, even to the point of monopolizing the strike. This was known to have resulted in many a heated exchange between the two. Most heinous of all his crimes, however, was probably a tendency to mock the Board of Control, specifically in a film he made of the 1948 tour to England and in newspaper articles on the 1950/51 MCC tour. The Australian authorities had always reacted strongly to the cricket/journalist. Before the war Arthur Mailey had been dismissed by New South Wales for writing the most inoffensive newspaper report of a match he was playing in. Even Bradman himself was fined £50 after the 1930 tour to England for a breach of the regulations. Keith Miller was similarly fined after the 1956 tour and the same issue recurs regularly down to the present day.

Matters came to a head in December 1951 when the Australian selectors chose Barnes for the third Test against the West Indians but the Board rejected his selection 'for reasons other than cricket'. There followed a conspiracy of silence in which nobody connected with the administration of Australian cricket would give any further explanation to the public or to Barnes.

It was not until eight months later that the facts came to light when Barnes sued a correspondent to the Sydney *Daily Mirror* who had sided with the Board on the issue. During the court case, the Board's minutes were subpoenaed and members were cross-examined. The trial was an overwhelming vindication for Barnes who, according to the defending council, 'was excluded [from the Australian team] on silly, trivial grounds'.

The case brought nothing but dishonour to the Australian Board and people began to openly question the right of administrators to act as judge and jury over players. Fingleton noted the international nature of the disease: 'Barnes looks like joining Eric Rowan of South Africa on cricket's list of unwanteds. Edrich is there too.' The *Evening Standard* commented: 'In these days sporting bodies take themselves more seriously and adopt a greater air of secrecy than the Cabinet of England.' And the *Daily Mail*: 'Too many cricket administrators in all parts of the world have become too dictatorial.'

The reference to Bill Edrich is an interesting one. In 1950, at the peak of his cricketing career, he was dropped from the England team during the series against the West Indies. A certain discomfort against the spin of Ramadhin and Valentine and a later injury obscured the real reason which was an astonishingly harsh disciplinary action by the authorities at Lord's. Apparently, during the penultimate evening of the Old Trafford Test match Edrich had been drinking in celebration of an expected victory on the next day. Bob Wyatt, one of the England selectors reported that this had affected his play and Edrich soon found himself summoned to report to a committee consisting of Colonel R. S. Rait Kerr, Pelham Warner, and H. S. Altham – the core of the so-called establishment. They told Edrich, in no uncertain terms, that he should make himself unavailable for selection to tour Australia during the coming winter – a tour for which he had originally been an outside contender for the captaincy. In the end he refused to withdraw but was simply not selected for the tour and, in fact, was essentially suspended from the England team for another three years.

This action seems somewhat harsh when viewed in retrospect and in a way the authorities were fortunate that Edrich did not publicly announce the facts of the case. In the more belligerent climate of the late fifties, the whole affair could so easily have erupted into an embarrassing and damaging media outcry. The clash seems to have been a classic example of an older generation with traditional values simply being on a different wavelength to a man like Edrich. He had been through a lot as a bomber pilot during the war, winning the DFC, and could perhaps have been excused for cherishing his moments of relaxation and enjoyment. Such behaviour would certainly be reprehensible in today's highly professional, highly paid international teams, but those were different times and Edrich – playing as an amateur – could surely have been forgiven. He was the type of person who gave every ounce of his energy – whether on the cricket field or during the after-match parties. It could well have been this case which led Godfrey Evans to say: 'These days in English cricket I have sometimes thought that it is what you do off the field that puts you on the field. Succeeding off the field and being in bed early seems to be one of the signposts to cricketing success.'

Clearly in these early post-war years, although many of the disciplinary actions must have been justified, there was still at least a hint of the old dictatorial attitude as far as the game's authorities were concerned, in both Australia and England. The method of punishment available to these authorities when a player was in disfavour were strictly limited. Fines or suspensions have never been fashionable in cricket until recently. When the

MCC or Australian Board were involved, we have seen that their only real weapon was the non-selection of individuals for Tests and tours. As far as county committees were concerned the solution was occasionally the extreme one of giving the player the sack. During the early fifties, the reasons for such disciplinary action were usually concerned with how a player behaved. Edrich and Barnes were prime examples, but Freddie Trueman, Tony Lock and others had good reason to think that they missed tours for reasons other than cricket ability. Both of these young players established something of a reputation during the troublesome 1953/4 tour to the West Indies and when they, in company with Jim Laker, were surprisingly omitted from the following winter's trip to Australia, the *Cricketer* magazine commented: 'Selectors have information and facts at their disposal which are not available to the general public . . . every avenue of form and temperament was closely examined.'

As the decade wore on a new reason for conflict arose. Cricketers began to incur the wrath of the authorities through a steadily increasing incidence of controversial written articles and books. We have seen how the journalistic efforts of Barnes, Miller and others had antagonized the Australian Board. In England the ghosted autobiographies of several players, published usually on their retirement, brought varying degrees of censure. Denis Compton in his book *End of an Innings* was unusually critical of Len Hutton. His Middlesex twin, Bill Edrich, raised a few hackles in his *Round the Wicket*. When read today, however, this all seems rather tame stuff and, over-exposed to sensation as we are, it is difficult to understand what all the fuss was about. There were other cases; we have already quoted from Tyson's autobiography and Neil Harvey had some remarkably vindictive comments to make in a series of newspaper articles after his retirement. These incidents were not sufficient to provoke any direct action by the authorities but two other examples were considered far more serious – the Wardle and Laker 'affairs'.

Johnny Wardle was an established England and Yorkshire player, thirty-five years old, when he became involved in a storm of controversy in the summer of 1958. In many ways he was one of the most talented players of the post-war era. A more than useful batsman and fielder, he was primarily a highly gifted bowler in the Sobers mould – left-arm orthodox spin, chinamen and googlies, or medium pace. As often as not he was preferred to Tony Lock in the England team and but for the latter's devastating but illegal faster ball he would probably have been an automatic first choice. In 1958 he was at the peak of his powers.

After an initial doubt as to whether he would make himself available to tour Australia in the coming winter of 1958/9, Wardle was eventually selected in July as a key member of the MCC party. Three days later the Yorkshire committee announced their bombshell – at the end of the year they would be dispensing with the services of Wardle. The reason, announced later by the committee, was that

> . . . in past years Wardle has been warned on several occasions that his general behaviour on the field and in the dressing-rooms left much to be desired. As no improvement was shown this year, the decision to dispense with his services was made, as it was unanimously considered that it was essential to have discipline and a happy and loyal team before any lasting improvement could be expected in the play of the Yorkshire XI.

This decision was probably part of a much wider problem in the Yorkshire team of the period. Various commentators close to the team have described the discordant atmosphere that prevailed. Whether this caused the lack of playing success during the fifties or whether it was a result is not sure. Certainly a stronger leadership might have been able to curb the excesses in temperament of the many individualists in the Yorkshire team. Norman Yardley was apparently too pleasant an individual to rule with the required rod of iron and his successor, Billy Sutcliffe, never had the authority to dominate the likes of Close, Trueman, Wardle, Watson and other seasoned professionals. Perhaps if Len Hutton had been captain for the entire decade after the war things might have been different. Anyway, J. M. Kilburn certainly believed that both Yardley and Hutton retired with a feeling of relief to be no longer involved in the atmosphere of the Yorkshire dressing-room.

Throughout the fifties there had been an unsettled feeling within Yorkshire cricket. In 1951, Alec Coxon was dismissed after taking 131 inexpensive wickets the previous season. The reason was apparently that his 'face did not fit'. Willie Watson, a gifted England batsman, left the county to become Leicestershire's captain when he felt that his development was being limited at Yorkshire. In 1958, Frank Lawson and Bob Appleyard, both England internationals, were also let go, but the greatest arguments surrounded Wardle.

For the next match after the announcement of his dismissal, Wardle requested that he stand down from the team because of articles that were to be published under his name in the *Daily Mail*. The articles proved to be a pretty crude attempt to cash in through the vilification of his Yorkshire team-mates, captain and committee members. The Yorkshire secretary announced that these articles simply 'justified the committee's decision' and Wardle's contract was terminated immediately. The distasteful outburst by Wardle turned public opinion almost totally against him. In addition, some counties who had made offers for his services saw fit to withdraw them. Still, for some time it did appear that he might sign for Nottinghamshire but this eventually fell through and he finished his career in the Lancashire leagues and playing for Cambridgeshire in the Minor Counties championship.

The publication of the articles automatically turned what had originally been considered a domestic affair into a matter for the MCC. After some lively public debate the authorities decided to withdraw Wardle's invitation to tour Australia because he had done 'a grave disservice to the game'. It was stated that, as well as the newspaper articles, they 'considered a report received from the Yorkshire County Cricket Club, many of the details of which were not available to the selection committee at the time when the team was chosen'.

This was clearly not a unanimous decision. Before the announcement, Peter May, the tour captain, had stated that he felt Wardle should still be included. Len Hutton agreed, adding that he had not found Wardle difficult to handle, just temperamental. Two years later, however, Godfrey Evans wrote, 'Len [Hutton] and Johnny Wardle did not hit it off either . . . but perhaps Len can't be blamed for that; not many people on tour have got on well with Johnny.' Alan Ross also admits Wardle's failings while basically siding with him in the dispute:

> Though he behaved subsequently with crazy and short-sighted impulsiveness, it was under much provocation, and, on any of his three MCC tours, he never put a foot wrong. He may not be the most genial or sociable of creatures, and I express my opinion here, not expecting it to be popular but merely practical.

The other equally infamous 'disservice to cricket' case was that of Jim Laker and the publication of his book *Over To Me*. This occurred in early 1960, just a few months after his initial retirement from first-class cricket and his subsequent election as an honorary MCC member. The book was an extreme catalogue of Laker's bitterness over a variety of events, and among the many targets Peter May, Freddie Brown and Desmond Eagar stood out. The first official reaction came from the Surrey Club, which withdrew Laker's pass to the ground, pavilion and dressing-rooms at The Oval. They clearly resented the fact that, so soon after receiving a benefit of £10,000, Laker had violently criticized the county and its players. The club secretary wrote to Laker as follows: 'There have been other books recently which lovers of cricket have regarded as harmful and in bad taste, but in the opinion of the committee yours has done a greater disservice to cricket than any of them.'

A short while later Mullers, the publishers of the book, issued a public apology to Bill Edrich, whose reputation as a cricketer-journalist was impugned in the text. Then, at the beginning of July, the MCC decided to cancel Laker's honorary membership. Since Laker had retired from cricket there was little else the game's authorities could do in the way of punishment. In a case like this, of course, the attendant publicity only serves two purposes – to increase the sales of the book and to further deteriorate the reputation of professional cricket and the people who play it.

In the long term, Laker's reputation was happily restored within the game. He wrote another book in which he expressed regret over the contents of the previous one – apparently the ghost writer was quite irresponsible – and he even returned to cricket as an amateur with Essex. Ultimately his privileges at The Oval and Lord's were returned and he has, of course, built a considerable reputation as a commentator on the game.

We have briefly described some of the trials and tribulations endured by Yorkshire cricket during the fifties, but they were far from the only club to suffer. During the infamous year of 1958, the committee of the Glamorgan County Club subjected itself to what Wilfred Wooller has described as 'an extraordinary period of madness'. Wooller himself was the centre of the controversy.

After twelve arduous years as both captain and secretary of the club, Wooller, at the age of forty-six, had decided to give up the playing side at the end of the 1958 season. Enquiries were started throughout the cricket world for an amateur replacement and an advertisement was even placed in the personal column of *The Times*. As 1958 wore on rumours circulated that Peter Richardson or Billy Sutcliffe might accept the post, and during August A. E. Burnett was specially registered and given a rather unsuccessful month's trial in the team. Burnett was a Cambridge blue who had not played since 1949 and would only be available while on sabbatical from his job as housemaster at Eton. He clearly was not worthy of a place in the team and the idea, a questionable one to begin with, was abandoned. Already, however, an atmosphere of intrigue had developed. Burnett was registered without Wooller's knowledge and he was felt by the players to be acting as a 'committee spy'.

Before this, however, a major behind-the-scenes row had blown up over the future role of Wooller. As captain/secretary he had been paid £900 per annum plus £100 expense allowance. In addition to this he received a steady income from journalism and broadcasting. When he announced his retirement as a player, however, the county committee offered to keep him on only as a part-time adviser at £500 per annum, plus £100 expenses. Immediately, it seemed, everybody associated with Glamorgan cricket became swept up in the argument and a clear split emerged. You were either pro-Wooller or pro-committee. Johnny Clay, one of the founding fathers of Glamorgan as a first-class team and a devoted club servant, resigned with the statement: 'I regard the decision about Wooller as a tragic blunder made by a committee out of a combination of ignorance and personal prejudice.' He later added that the committee had been wet-nursed by successive captains in Turnbull and Wooller, and that, 'Without Wooller, Glamorgan will be like a ship without a rudder.' Further resignations were made, members signed petitions, Wooller offered to stay on for another year, but still the committee were resolute in their determination to get rid of him. The entire episode was characterized by intrigue and cloak and dagger activities, many of which were played out in the full glare of newspaper publicity. Finally, a referendum of the club members gave resounding support for Wooller and the chairman of twenty-five years' standing, Colonel J. M. Bevan, resigned (with ten other committee members) with the simple parting statement, 'Wilfred Wooller will now manage the club.' In fact, he stayed on as captain for two more seasons before finally handing over to Ossie Wheatley and remaining as full-time secretary. It is interesting to compare this episode with the more recent Boycott case in Yorkshire. Some intriguing parallels exist and Wooller clearly set a precedent for Boycott's victory over the incumbent committee.

At the time, the whole affair was very bitter. During the referendum one committee member was served with a writ because he was giving people the impression that Wooller had milked the club expenses. Wooller even considered libel action when some disgusting attacks were made impugning his private life. After a year or two, it was clear that the club had emerged unscathed but the damage in terms of cricket's prestige could never be undone. This was just one more in the steady stream of issues which put cricket in the headlines for reasons totally unrelated to the field of play.

Lancashire were another county who seemed to become frequently entangled with internal strife that brought little credit to the game in general. Here again the issue was mainly one of poor communication between players and club officials. The team captaincy was another factor at the heart of many of the club squabbles. This really started in 1947 when the popular and successful Jack Fallows was relieved of the captaincy and replaced by the unknown Ken Cranston, much to the consternation of most of the team. John Kay, the county historian, observed that: 'It opened a gulf between players and committee which widened as the years passed by until it reached a stage when there was almost open rebellion between those who administered and those who played.'

Cranston, of course, quickly became a firm favourite at Old Trafford and was a highly successful captain. Similarly, his successor Nigel Howard surprised many with his abilities despite his lack of experience when first introduced to leadership in 1949. Initially it appeared that everything was against him. The senior professionals, suspicious by now of the rapid turnover in amateur captains, were pointedly unhelpful to the young newcomer and were initially content to see what sort of a mess he would make of the job. Unfortunately, Howard did receive an abundance of advice, but from the wrong sources. The club chairman, the secretary (who was Howard's father) and his mother were continually directing the new captain with regard to on-the-field decisions. During away games poor Howard would repeatedly receive urgent telegrams from these helpers with detailed instructions including even specific bowling changes. One can imagine that this type of thing hardly encouraged a good team spirit, but to Howard's credit he overcame the handicaps and finished as a pretty good skipper.

When a professional, Cyril Washbrook, was finally appointed to the captaincy Lancashire could boast a strong team and might reasonably have been expected to win the championship during the mid-fifties. One of the players of this period lays the blame for the lack of success squarely on the captain and the unsettled atmosphere in the dressing-room created by the autocratic nature of the committee:

> I am certain if we had had the right skipper at this time we would have won the championship two or three times. The players felt very remote from the committee at this time, just replaceable employees. The problem on a large committee as we had at Old Trafford, say thirty on the committee, was that seventeen knew nothing about cricket but could sway the issue.

By the end of the decade the county's problems were more severe, if anything, and still revolved around the committee's relationship with the captain and his team. Washbrook had been replaced on his retirement by the highly gifted but inexperienced Cambridge blue Bob Barber. He was thrown in at the deep end and his unfortunate experiences very nearly ruined a highly promising career. In the end, a change of counties was necessary before Barber blossomed into a spectacular opening batsman for England and Warwickshire.

The relationship between Barber and the county really blew up in August 1960 when Kent refused Barber's challenge to score 334 runs to win in 265 minutes on an easy wicket and against an attack lacking the services of Brian Statham. After the game, Barber announced to the press that he was 'fed up' with the way county cricket was being played and disgusted with the action of Colin Cowdrey, the Kent captain. He added: 'I consider I gave Cowdrey and Kent a fair chance of winning and my side an equally fair chance of doing the same, but the challenge was ignored. Lancashire will never do the same under my captaincy.' Cowdrey, quite sensibly, refused to get involved in a public argument and contented himself with the comment: 'I don't believe mud-slinging and cricket go together.'

It was at this point that the Lancashire committee took a hand in the proceedings. Geoffrey Howard, the club secretary, issued the statement that, 'Lancashire CCC is in no way associated with the opinions of its captain.' This type of thing was hardly likely to instil loyalty in the players and indeed the club members started a petition deploring the fact that Barber had not been supported by the committee. In the end Barber quite rightly apologized for the personal nature of the attack on Cowdrey, but his days at Old Trafford were numbered. He eventually left the club and was replaced as captain by an unknown club cricketer, Joe Blackledge. Needless to say the move hardly improved the stormy nature of the county fortunes. Some first team players were dismissed from the club or left to join other counties and the whole atmosphere simply added fire to cricket's declining public image at this time.

Clearly this period saw a drastic change in the attitude of players and supporters toward the unquestioning acceptance of the sometimes ill-informed and dictatorial decisions of county committees. The troubles at Yorkshire, Glamorgan and Lancashire were possibly the most visible cases but they were symptomatic of a pretty widespread trend. Cricket's dirty linen was being washed in the full gaze of an eager public, and while the popular press revelled in the disease the long term effects on the game's image were extremely detrimental. The effect was even more startling because cricket, above all other sports, had represented all the traditional virtues. Dating from those few years in the late fifties, the phrase 'it isn't cricket' would begin to have a slightly hollow ring.

Another county which laid itself open to trial by newspaper was Gloucestershire. Their much publicized row with Tom Graveney came at the end of 1960, hot on the heels of the Laker, Barber and throwing controversies of that summer. Again, it was a case of heavy-handed behaviour by the county committee, which clearly did not anticipate that a mere paid employee, Graveney, would show any dissent against their decisions. Very few amateurs had appeared for Gloucestershire in the fifties and the county had, therefore, had a succession of professional captains in Crapp, Emmett and Graveney. The side had been pretty successful during the latter's two years of leadership, finishing second in 1959 and eighth in 1960. It was, therefore, something of a shock when Graveney was dismissed as captain but, as the player himself has said, it was the manner in which the decision was made which really upset him:

On 18 November the club announced that one of our young

amateurs, Tom Pugh, had been appointed Captain. No mention of me or my position was made in the club announcement, and I was neither consulted nor officially advised of the action. Last month [November] I was told for the first time that when I was appointed captain in 1959, the club's policy even then was to have an amateur captain at some future date.

There were two main points to the case. Firstly, the Gloucestershire committee clearly felt it unnecessary to do Graveney the courtesy of discussing the situation and explaining their position. This can perhaps be explained as a simple case of very poor communication and a rather out-dated reappearance of the dictatorial attitude by administrators. Secondly, and perhaps more disturbingly, was the aspect that even as late as 1960 the committee was determined to have an amateur captain, even one as unsuccessful as Pugh, no matter how well Graveney performed. This is confirmed by E. W. Swanton, who relates in his autobiography how a Gloucestershire official told him back in 1959 that they were grooming Pugh to take over. When Swanton expressed surprise at the thought of replacing Graveney, he was told: 'Oh, I don't think there would be any trouble. The pros don't like the responsibility very much, you know, they're happier without it.'

At it happened, that official could not have been further from the truth and 'trouble' is exactly what did happen. Graveney was naturally very bitter and resigned from the club immediately. Faced with losing their most outstanding cricketer the county tried to placate Graveney but the ill-feeling ran too deep to be forgiven and he joined Worcestershire. The county tried to justify their decision by saying that Graveney was dismissed because the team 'deprecated his authority', but the overwhelming weight of public sympathy clearly went to Graveney. This was just one more incident that occurred in the painful period of transition before the less enlightened of the game's authorities realized that modern professionals were human beings who deserved, and indeed demanded, to be treated as equals.

Beyond the domestic boundaries of county cricket other sources of controversy which increasingly brought the game into disrepute were international tours. Under an ever increasing glare of publicity the modern norm of incident and sensation gradually took over. The captain of a touring team is, of course, intimately involved with any incident but beyond that the role of

England's captain has been a continual source of intrigue. The post-war England captains, particularly on overseas tours, have had a far more exacting task than did their predecessors. Not only have they been concerned with the actual cricket but, partly due to the changes in the attitudes and social position of the professional cricketer, it has not always been easy to achieve a harmonious tour. In the early post-war years this was especially a problem.

Things were off to a pretty bad start with the first MCC post-war tour to Australia, under the leadership of Wally Hammond, a truly great cricketer but by all accounts a rather average captain. The tour was billed as a goodwill mission and went ahead despite MCC reservations about the weakness of English cricket so soon after the war. In the end, England were badly beaten but there were certainly huge crowds and much good was achieved by the tour. Within the England party, however, there was very little goodwill. In fact, many of the players felt considerable animosity towards the way in which Hammond and the tour manager, Rupert Howard, conducted the tour. Poor Hammond did not have a good time with the bat and since his personal life was undergoing the agony of a divorce it is perhaps not surprising that he paid little attention to the needs of his team. He even became embroiled in a personal feud with his rival captain, Bradman, and throughout the series they hardly spoke to each other except to call 'heads' or 'tails'.

Off the field, the tour had an incredible start when Brian Sellers, the Yorkshire captain who was in Australia as a journalist, wrote an article to the effect that Hammond was tactically inept and was certainly not the man to captain England. While this may have been true it was a strange statement in light of the fact that Sellers had been a member of the tour selection committee! Probably the most honest comments on Hammond's behaviour during this tour are to be found in Paul Gibb's diary, recently published in *Wisden Cricket Monthly*. In answer to the Sellers article, Sir Pelham Warner was quoted as saying that Hammond had one of the greatest brains in cricket. Gibb wrote, with a fine sense of understatement: 'Great player as the Skipper is, and much as he is to be admired in many ways, I think it is doubtful whether his cricket brain has quite the quality credited to it by Sir Pelham.'

The major problem in the touring party seemed to be that Hammond, who was head and shoulders above the rest in seniority and stature in the game, appeared to be aloof from his younger team-mates. In this he was encouraged rather than counselled by Howard, the manager. Hammond had been loaned a beautiful Jaguar car for the duration of the tour and these two would travel in it, separate from the team, whenever possible. By Christmas everybody in the team seemed to be complaining about what Gibb described as Hammond's 'apparently complete lack of interest in the welfare of the team'. Later in the tour Gibb had to undergo an operation to remove an ulcer from his head. In his diary he wrote:

> It is worth noting that neither the captain, Wally Hammond, nor the manager, Rupert Howard, has so far evidenced the slightest interest in my condition. Not that I care a button. But I think that if I was captain of a side I should show a little more interest in the players under me. It was the same when Peter Smith was operated upon. After the first game in which he played after coming from the hospital neither captain nor manager so much as asked how he felt. Extraordinary.

Although this type of behaviour would have brought resentment at any time it is probably true to say that after the war people were less likely to stand for these types of perceived injustice. The days in which the leaders of a tour could separate themselves from the rest of the players into an aloof clique were over. The generation gap also played a major role in the earlier post-war tours. Due to the six missing cricket years teams tended to be polarized into the old pre-war hands and a new group of relative youngsters. Godfrey Evans, then a young man on his first tour, said of Hammond: 'He was unpopular with some members of the side, not without reason, because he appeared to arrange things for his own convenience . . . he rarely asked for advice. He hardly ever gave praise.'

The strength of feeling that built up during this long and arduous tour is best summed up by the following caustic epitaph from Paul Gibb:

> This is the day upon which any active participation in the trip as a member of England's 1946/7 team to tour Australia came to an end. Somehow I feel a new man with a sense of greater freedom. Free from what, I don't exactly know. Free, perhaps, from an ever-present awareness of my erstwhile skipper's presence, free from his unfathomable, quite unpredictable

and rather untrustworthy moods. I wouldn't trust Wally
Hammond any further than I can see him.

Of course, this is only one side of the case – maybe Hammond in
turn found Gibb to be a strange tourist. Nevertheless, it is fair to
conclude that this tour was characterized by internal strife, most
of which was kept out of the contemporary newspapers. The
conflicts were due to personality clashes, poor communications
and just plain bad leadership. The next trouble-filled tour, the
1953/4 MCC visit to the West Indies, was altogether different in
character. Here, every scandal and controversy was put under
the microscope of the press and the blueprint for so many of our
modern tours was set.

Alex Bannister, in his book on the tour, summed up the
atmosphere as follows:

> Almost from first to last a wave of prejudice, acrimony and
> undesirable bitterness made the tour the most unpleasant and
> unfortunate experience in cricket since the visit of
> D. R. Jardine's MCC team to Australia in 1932/3.

The list of reasons for this unhappy assessment reads like a
catalogue of modern cricket problems:

> Umpiring – a poor standard exacerbated by intimidation and
> resulting in complaints by the tourists
> Crowd trouble
> Poor player behaviour, both on and off the field
> Excessive short-pitched fast bowling
> Slow over-rate
> Defensive tactics – leg stump attack

As on the 1946/7 tour, much of the blame for these problems has
been placed at the door of the captain and manager – in this case
Len Hutton and Charles Palmer. One of the most disturbing new
developments was the reported incidence of ungentlemanly
behaviour by some of the England players. A host of off-the-field
incidents were rumoured, many of which were doubtless untrue
or exaggerated. The fact remains, though, that Freddie
Trueman's good-conduct bonus was withheld by the MCC and
he was passed over for future international honours for several
years. The allegations of unfriendly and even offensive behaviour
towards the West Indian players seemed to stem from Hutton's
insistence on a grim, give-no-quarter, tough attitude. This did
not sit well with some of the more easy-going English players.
Godfrey Evans wrote: 'I don't think Len helped matters much . . .

"we've got to do 'em. You mustn't speak to 'em on or off the field" . . . I think he made a big contribution to the sharpness and acrimony of that most controversial of tours.' Denis Compton added: 'Len Hutton's attitude quickly made things a good deal worse.' Hutton, of course, was under intense pressure and scrutiny. This was the first time a professional had led an MCC side on a major overseas tour and there were plenty of traditionalists waiting in the wings to say that a pro could not handle the social and man-management demands of a tour. While there was much ammunition for these detractors, Hutton finally saved his reputation by virtue of a series of superhuman personal batting performances which rescued the playing record of the team. Also it was felt that the lack of discipline in the tour party was partly the fault of the easy-going nature of manager Palmer. E. W. Swanton even went as far as to describe his appointment as 'in my experience, just about the worst decision ever to have come out of Lord's.'

Another feature which started on this tour, and continued during the rest of Hutton's captaincy, was the use of the slow over-rate as a deliberate tactic to frustrate the opposition. This was part of the grim, warlike attitude that Hutton instilled and which brought a dullness to much of the play in the fifties. To lay the blame on Hutton is somewhat unfair, however, since he was probably reacting to the humiliating beatings England had suffered before his term as captain. He had known the relentlessness of Bradman, who had in turn been toughened by his experience of Jardine, so the trend was in many ways inherited. Nevertheless it has grown into the most insidious disease of modern cricket.

There were other tours in this period that had their share of controversy but by far the most acrimonious topic was the throwing issue. This whole subject has been traced historically in an entire book by Ian Peebles, but it certainly came to a climax during those tumultuous years of discord between 1958 and 1960. Firstly, the 1958/9 MCC tour to Australia was ruined by the bad feeling caused by the doubtful actions of Meckiff and a host of others. It seemed that the problem had germinated almost overnight in Australian domestic cricket. There were problems in the West Indies and in England but the most ignominious spectacle occurred during the 1960 South African tour to England when the infamous Griffin was so sadly exposed at Lord's. In some ways this sudden eruption of throwing was a reflection of a certain laxness or permissiveness in cricket. Throwers only reached international cricket because of the tolerance of coaches, selectors and administrators throughout the world. When they were successful, like Tony Lock, their transgressions tended to be winked at by the authorities.

Happily, the crisis was finally dealt with, mainly due to the brave and sweeping actions taken by Australia, under the leadership of Sir Donald Bradman. Nevertheless, the scars were permanently left behind on this most troubled of cricket eras.

As well as the throwing crisis, many of the other undesirable features of international tours also seemed to be put aside during the early sixties. The influence of the West Indians, Richie Benaud, Walter Robins and others has been dealt with in the chapter on so-called 'Brighter Cricket', but there was one controversy which was only just beginning to stir during these years. This was to ultimately become, and remain to this day, the most emotional and contentious of all cricket's talking-points – the South African question.

Although the most trouble-filled years regarding South African cricket connections came after the d'Oliveira affair in 1968, the seeds had been sown much earlier. The 1960 South African tour to England involved the first serious public demonstrations against such sporting encounters and thereby constitute the background to much which has followed. Prior to that tour the desirability of playing cricket against a country which treated non-white citizens so abominably had never really been discussed. Segregation had been practised in South African domestic cricket since Victorian times but the rest of the world took little interest. The average cricket fan rarely questioned why South Africa never played against the West Indies, India or Pakistan. Players on MCC tours to South Africa were typically kept away from the more sordid aspects of life and, almost to a man, they reported that the country was a paradise on earth. Just occasionally a more deep-thinking individual would see what was really happening and decide that he had no wish to visit a country where human rights were so flagrantly violated. John Arlott reported the 1948/9 MCC tour but afterwards decided he would not return. Some of the English county players who coached in the Republic during the fifties had more opportunity to see the attitudes towards non-whites and stories would occasionally filter back to their colleagues. By and large, however, the cricket world – players, administrators and spectators – neither knew nor cared about apartheid.

It was in 1960 that this situation really began to change. There was very little in the way of demonstration or disruption during the tour itself, but in the months leading up to the arrival of the South African team the first rumbles of protest were heard. They seem mild by comparison with what has followed – the d'Oliveira affair, the 'Stop the 1970 Tour' campaign, and the tour by 'Gooch's rebels' – but 1960 marked the beginning of public awareness that the issue existed. In January the Rev. N. D. Stacey, a vicar in Birmingham and former Olympic athlete, announced his refusal to attend a 'Sportsmen's Service' to be held in the summer and to be attended by the South African team. Later, in the spring, the Welsh mineworkers' union asked that Glamorgan cancel their fixture with the South African tourists. By far the most prominent protest, however – certainly as far as the newspapers were concerned – was the announcement by the Rev. David Sheppard that he had refused to appear for the Duke of Norfolk's eleven in their opening match against the South African tourists. In his autobiography, *Parson's Pitch*, Sheppard has described the background to this action, which he felt obliged to make on moral grounds. He had made the decision as early as January but wanted to delay the public announcement until after his resignation from the MCC committee in May. In the end, Sheppard's stand became public knowledge in early April, at a time when events in South Africa were filling every newspaper headline in the world. The infamous Sharpeville massacre, when sixty-seven Africans were killed by the police, was the most prominent in a series of riots which brought about an official state of emergency in the Republic. Jackie McGlew's touring team set foot in England at the height of this publicity and were greeted by the Sheppard story and 500 protestors waiting for them at London Airport.

For a while public opinion was at fever pitch. Hugh Gillespie, a South African rugby league player who played for York, was forced to return home because of 'increased animosity towards South Africans in this country'. There were frequent rumours. Worcestershire had to publicly announce that their two black players – Ron Headley and Laddie Outschoorn – would certainly be considered for the tourists' first county fixture. In May, fifty-six Oxford dons wrote to the secretary of the University cricket club protesting against the upcoming match with the South Africans. Matters soon cooled down, however, and there was never the sort of sustained or organized protest of later years.

The cricket 'establishment', perhaps somewhat predictably, reacted to these protests with an indignant horror. The *Cricketer* magazine, in a review of Charles Fortune's tour book, stated that the tour began with

> . . . political agitations against a team of cricketers who of all people were least deserving of reproach. Indeed, the very fact that there should be bad feeling in connection with the traditionally sporting South Africans would seem to bode ill for cricket. It is therefore natural for Mr Fortune to wax indignant – especially after receiving abusive letters from barbarians.

E. W. Swanton summarized the feelings of many when he stated that the protests were wrong because the touring cricketers never expressed their support of apartheid. The now familiar cry against bringing politics into sport was expressed many times. It has been a common trait in cricketing circles to treat the game as a separate, almost sacred entity. It is one of the main principles of this book, however, that cricket is an integral part of society and is deeply influenced by developments in the world at large. By this token, it is impossible to separate politics from cricket. Certainly in the case of South Africa the connection was made not by the protestors but by the South African government. The country practised apartheid not only in work and education but in the playing of all sports. Politics and sport were already mixed in South Africa before ever a single protest was heard in England. This interdependence is nothing new; from Hitler's use of the 1936 Olympics for propaganda, to Nixon's 'ping-pong diplomacy' with Red China, it has been a fact of life. As far back as 1908 Britain demanded that the Finnish team march under a Russian flag at the Olympics because a trade pact had just been signed between the UK and Russia. More recently, in 1973, the French government banned a sports engagement in Australia after a row over French nuclear tests in the Pacific. There is a depressingly long list of other examples.

One footnote to the South African issue is of special interest in light of the recent rebel West Indian tours of that country. In November 1958, it was announced that a team of black West Indian Test players, captained by Frank Worrell, would tour South Africa subject to their obtaining entrance visas. In March of the following year the South African government gave approval for the tour as long as they only played against non-whites and that separate seating and other facilities be made for white and non-white spectators. This brought a protest from many of the coloured cricketing fraternity in South Africa since acceptance of such terms by Worrell's team would be tantamount to condoning apartheid. In the end the tour was cancelled after strong requests from the Indian Cricket Board and the idea remained dormant for more than twenty years before resurfacing in 1982.

To summarize this chapter, the trend towards increased controversy within the game can be rationalized in the context of overall social trends. After the war there was a gradual but distinct change in values; the old codes of behaviour were cast aside and a new era of permissiveness was ushered in. In concert with this came a move away from the traditional acceptance of authority. Protests, demonstrations, strikes and a certain amount of dissatisfaction were part and parcel of everyday life and these features were highlighted by a more definable generation gap and increased media coverage. Cricket reflected these changes, and many of the issues which brought the game into disrepute stemmed from the new attitudes towards authority. Cricket in England suffered most from these troubles during three hectic years from 1958 to 1960. In that period the following scandals all made newspaper headlines:

August 1958	Wardle affair
August-December 1958	Wooller/Glamorgan dispute
	Denis Compton autobiography critical of Hutton
November 1958-March 1959	MCC's 'Throwing Tour' to Australia
March 1959	Frank Worrell's book accuses English players of ungentlemanly conduct
April 1959	Peter Richardson leaves Worcestershire amid controversy and must miss twelve months' cricket
April 1960	Protests over South African tour
May 1960	Laker's book published and later his MCC membership withdrawn
June 1960	Griffin (S.A.) no-balled for throwing during Lord's Test Match

| June 1960 | Young fast bowler dismissed by Worcestershire for stealing from fellow players. Later to become highly successful county cricketer. |
| December 1960 | Graveney sacked as Gloucestershire captain. Leaves the county and forced to miss twelve months' cricket. |

Since then, of course, there has been a steady stream of similar controversies. So far cricket has been fortunate in avoiding the ultimate folly – a strike by professional players. Recently American football and baseball have both been disrupted in this way and the result was a considerable degree of public disillusionment with the players. Hopefully this will be avoided in cricket, but the increasing presence of large monetary rewards for players makes the likelihood of such a dispute that much closer. Indeed, during 1973 Tony Greig apparently urged the Players' Association to institute a sit-down protest during three successive Sunday League matches. The protest, which never materialized, was aimed at securing a greater share of TV revenues for the players.

As nearly always in cricket history, there are precedents for industrial action by professional cricketers. As long ago as 1881 seven of the finest players in the great Nottinghamshire team of the period – including Shaw, Shrewsbury and Barnes – refused to play for the county unless their demands were met. The players were seeking a guaranteed benefit and the right to organize their own matches. In neither case were they successful and the County Club took the strongest possible line to quash the uprising. Another example was in 1896 when five of the England team – Richardson, Lohmann, Abel, Hayward and Gunn – demanded a payment of £20 for appearing in a Test Match as opposed to the £10 offered. Again, the county concerned (Surrey) reacted sharply and the attempt at 'player power' was ended almost before it had begun.

Of course, the Packer entanglement (see Chapter 9) of the late seventies was a modern version of such actions but on a super scale. Whether it will be the last such action remains to be seen but the omens are not good judging by developments in other sports.

7
The Players

We have discussed the disappearance of the old-style amateur from county cricket but what of the players who took their place – the post-war professional cricketers? One danger in a book of this type is to talk of cricketers in terms of generalities, as if they are a series of stereotypes that can be neatly pigeon-holed. In reality, of course, as in any other walk of life, the profession of cricketer is made up of an infinite variety of individuals. Their backgrounds, dispositions, intellects and lives are unique. John Arlott has written,

> A survey of eminent cricketers would include statesmen, generals, barristers, peers, novelists, painters, music-hall entertainers, miners, farm-labourers, professional boxers, policemen and publicans.

Nevertheless, it should be possible to recognize some overall trends; while every player's personality may be different, many cricket careers have run along similar paths, largely determined by the characteristics of the game itself and of the social setting in which it is played. Both of these factors underwent dramatic change in the post-war era, so we would expect the cricketers and their careers to be broadly different from their predecessors.

A major factor which dominated the cricketers of the forties and fifties was, of course, the cessation of first-class cricket between 1939 and 1945. The war interrupted cricket careers in many different ways. Some, like Bradman and Hammond, had already achieved all the greatness the game can offer but were destined to return six years later to perform one last encore – in many ways a satisfying conclusion. Many others, like Compton, Hutton and Bill Edrich, were beginning to show every indication of emulating or even eclipsing the great players of the twenties and thirties. They were young enough to return and dominate the post-war years but forever the question will be asked, 'What would they have achieved in those six missing years when an athlete is at his peak?' Then one comes to the third category, the ones who were on the brink of first-class cricket in 1939. Many simply never again found the circumstances or determination to break into post-war cricket.

This wartime interruption also had a significant adverse effect on the standard of play in England, particularly with respect to the older bowlers. Many of the leading pre-war batsmen were young enough to continue but good bowlers were in short supply. In addition many of the post-war newcomers shone initially but subsequently failed to make the grade perhaps because of the loss of those vital early development years.

As well as this erosion of available talent caused by the war, other factors seriously limited the recruitment of players in the late forties. The post-war industrial manpower crisis almost had an equivalent in cricket. The Control of Engagement Order limited the counties to engaging three categories of player: those under the age of eighteen; those who were leaving the forces; and those already playing professional cricket. Since at the age of eighteen the majority were claimed for two years' National Service, the recruitment of promising youngsters was virtually impossible. Only in exceptional cases could a man be taken from employment in agriculture, mining or production industries. G. A. Smithson, a bright young prospect with Yorkshire in 1947, was given special leave by the Minister of Labour to join the MCC winter tour to the West Indies. Smithson, who was a 'Bevin Boy', was only released from work at the mines on the condition that he return to Askern Colliery after the tour. The following summer Ken Preston, a highly promising young fast bowler, was only allowed to join the Essex staff after receiving approval from the same Minister.

National Service claimed approximately 160,000 young people each year and was not abolished until 1960. This meant that during cricket's post-war recovery period and throughout the fifties each county typically had two or three of its brightest prospects absent at any given time. The Service cricket teams certainly benefited. In the early fifties players like Trueman, Titmus, Barrington, Parks, Illingworth, May, Close and a host of others were playing for the Army, Navy or Air Force when they could have been sharpening their skills in the County Championship. Some of these young cricketers probably suffered a setback by their tour of duty; Brian Close certainly seemed to fall back from the heights of his debut season in 1949. Others were encouraged and physically developed by the experience. Brian Statham had never seriously played cricket before the age of eighteen and had his first real chance in the RAF. Unfortunately, it was virtually impossible to escape National Service no matter how prominent a sportsman one might be. Yorkshire tried to argue that Freddie Trueman was exempt because he worked as a miner at Maltby Main colliery, but the Ministry of Labour was not impressed by the fact that he did not work there during the summer. Some people thought that Colin Cowdrey had escaped because of special influence, and, in fact, questions were raised in the House of Commons. Cowdrey was declared medically unfit for service but this raised eyebrows as it coincided with his triumphant first tour of Australia. One member stated that if he was fit enough to undertake such a strenuous athletic event then surely he was fit enough to peel potatoes in the RAF. In his autobiography, however, Cowdrey goes into the details of his case and makes a convincing argument that he was much maligned over the whole issue.

Anyway, the combined effects of the missing war years, Control of Engagement and National Service radically affected the pool of players available for county cricket. This was exacerbated by certain socio-economic developments of the period. There was generally high employment of an increasingly rewarding type. Education was typically being continued to a later age and, in particular, more youngsters went on to further education after leaving school. With the economic facts of life militating against the amateur, the game was just not competitive enough in attracting new professionals. The dramatic increase in education also required more teachers and this must have helped to remove potential cricketers from consideration.

Perhaps the best way to illustrate the trends in post-war cricketers' careers is to describe in 'snapshot' fashion some of the characters who have appeared on the county circuit. While none of them will be demeaned with the description 'typical', hopefully some generalization can be made of the changes during the period.

Turning first to the memorable 1947 season, the personalities who dominated that summer certainly evoke the 'feel' of a unique time in cricket history. One perceives an impression of an era totally foreign to that of the 1980s. The leading characters on show were, of course, the Middlesex 'twins' Compton and Edrich, both of whom broke the old record for highest run aggregate in a single season. For many, 1947 has blurred into the single memory of constant sunshine and these two batting throughout the afternoon. Widely contrasting in style and temperament, the careers of both men had some similarities. Both burst onto the cricket scene with no need of the traditional English apprenticeship. By the age of nineteen Compton had scored a century in a Test Match against Australia, whereas Edrich scored 2000 runs in his first full season, followed by a 1000 before the end of May in his second. Both were also highly capable bowlers – Compton took seventy-three wickets in 1947 and Edrich opened the bowling for England. Both were good soccer players at outside-left, although Edrich never achieved the success of Compton at the professional level. Most frustratingly, they are the two perfect examples of a generation of cricketers who had their finest years taken by the war. The full significance of this is not always appreciated. Cricket was the profession of these people, and when an active working lifespan might be only twenty years at most, the loss of six is no small sacrifice. In Compton's case his public prominence assured him of meaningful employment after he retired from cricket, but what of others who, like him, had joined the MCC ground staff at the age of fourteen but were never to become household names? Of course, the Welfare State ensured that we would never be faced with the occasional horror stories of earlier cricket generations.

The season of 1947 was poorer than its predecessor in only one way and that was the absence of Wally Hammond, who had surprisingly retired from cricket after the disappointing Australian tour of the previous winter. Hammond was, of course, the pre-eminent English batsman of the thirties and even in 1946 had dominated the scene with an average of 84.90. His sudden departure left the way open for Compton and Edrich to dominate the headlines and provide the batting power to the England team.

Although one thinks of 1947 as a batsman's season, Tom Goddard, the fiercely aggressive Gloucestershire off spinner, took 238 wickets – still the most in a post-war season and likely to remain so. Goddard performed this feat at the age of forty-six and this longevity in the game is another feature of cricket which was to gradually change throughout the fifties and sixties, before one-day cricket finally sealed the fate of the over-forties. Ahead of Goddard in the first-class averages came J. C. Clay of Glamorgan at the even more venerable age of forty-nine. The forty-five-year-old Arthur Wellard was still able to take good wickets, and there were a host of capable batsmen in the over-forties category, led by Bob Wyatt who at the age of forty-six still had a few good years to go in his career.

At the other end of the age spectrum, several new 'prospects' appeared this season, the first batch of the post-war newcomers who, despite their youth, had still experienced war-time interruption to their cricketing development. One such was Maurice Tremlett, who played his first game for Somerset against the all-conquering Middlesex team at Lord's. A powerful, strong man his efforts with bat and ball virtually won the match and he received glowing opinions all round, resulting in successive MCC tours to the West Indies (1947/48) and South Africa (1948/49). Unfortunately his promise was never really fulfilled, although in an unlucky career he became a useful, often exciting player and an excellent county captain – the first professional one for Somerset. He had been almost twenty-four by the time he left the Services and first played for the county, and these formative years could never be regained.

Another who never fulfilled the promise of his first season was David Fletcher of Surrey. In his first two championship games he scored 65, 46 and 194 and went on to appear for the Players, but was never to enjoy another season as successful as this, his first at the age of twenty-three. Others, of course, achieved greatness despite the war-time delay in their careers. Jim Laker made his first championship appearances in 1947 at the age of twenty-five and finished with 79 wickets at 17.97. Since, in the previous season, the Bedsers (aged twenty-eight) and Tony Lock (only seventeen) had made their debuts, this year completed the nucleus of the great Surrey bowling sides of the fifties.

Several amateur players of the old style played in 1947, although their numbers were greatly diminished compared to the between-wars period. One of the best was M. M. Walford, an old Oxford blue and Rugby international who played for Somerset only during the school holidays since he was a teacher at Sherbourne. In the second half of that summer his dashing, front-foot driving style, reminiscent of the Golden Age, brought him successive scores of 96, 52*, 90, 101 and 264. But the true amateur, displacing when he felt like it a man who relied on cricket for his income, was rapidly becoming an anachronism. We have seen that increased professionalism was a natural consequence of the times, and even the amateurs of the fifties were virtually full-time cricketers. Only a few such as J. G. Dewes, G.

H. G. Doggart and J. R. Thompson, maintained the schoolmaster tradition during the fifties, and, prominent though they were as cricketers, their part-time performances surely suffered in the new professional game.

Another remarkable amateur appeared on the scene in 1947. Kenneth Cranston, of Lancashire, played only two seasons of first-class cricket, but during that time his rise to fame was meteoric and the impression he made was universally favourable. Appointed as an unknown new captain of Lancashire he was selected for England after only thirteen county games and in his second Test match took four wickets in six balls. Only D. W. Carr (1909) and D. B. Close (1949) have similarly appeared for England in their very first season. Chosen to tour the West Indies the following winter, he captained England during G. O. Allen's absence. After the 1948 season he dropped out of first-class cricket altogether, in order to practise dentistry in Liverpool, and so an exciting and truly gifted player was lost to the game. In those two years Cranston scored 2000 runs, took almost 200 wickets, held nearly fifty catches, appeared in eight Tests, and never appeared to exert himself more than he would playing on a village green. Again this was to be one of the last glimpses of the old-style amateur rendered obsolete in the New Age.

Another newcomer county captain in 1947 was Derbyshire's Eddie Gothard, although there the similarity with Cranston ends. Aged forty-two, never more than a club player, and looking somewhat unathletic with spectacles taped to his temples with sticking plaster, he nevertheless served as a good captain. By the time of the vital August match with championship leaders Middlesex, Gothard had taken only one wicket in first-class cricket but, in desperation and the absence of Gladwin and Copson on Test duty, he not only bowled in this match but took a hat-trick including the prized wicket of Bill Edrich.

The fact that forty-two-year-old club players could command places in the county championship argues forcibly that the standard of cricket in the forties was very much below that which has followed. Indeed, writing in 1947, H. S. Altham said, 'The out-cricket in much that passes for first-class cricket is little short of lamentable.' The charm of stories like Gothard's, however, and the excitement and sheer enjoyment of the cricket in 1947 are enough to convince many that cricket has not profited by its increased uniformity and level of skill.

Much of the credit for the enjoyment in the cricket of the late forties must go to the county captains. The most prominent was Walter Robins, who led Middlesex to the championship by an all-out attacking policy, never afraid to take a risk in the quest for victory. On the hard, dusty pitches of a sun-baked August the Middlesex bowling attack sometimes contained five spinners, three of them leg spinners (Robins and Sims, the pre-war Test players, and Ian Bedford, a seventeen-year-old grammar school boy) and one (Compton) a left-handed wrist spinner. A match in which these players were concerned could never be dull. Bedford was another who never rose again to his youthful achievements after a two year spell of National Service.

Another remorselessly attacking county captain was Wilfred Wooller, who was to lead Glamorgan to an historic championship in 1948. A former Welsh Rugby international and recent Japanese prisoner of war, he was a persistent all-rounder, astute captain and, above all, a fierce competitor. Soon, Stuart Surridge was to follow this aggressive, attacking style of leadership, but gradually throughout the fifties it was to be the more conservative approach, exemplified by Hutton's handling of the England team, that would come to dominate, and in some ways stifle, cricket.

Although it is tempting to emphasize the careers and performances of the most famous Test Match players, a study such as this would be incomplete without consideration of the so-called 'average' county cricketer. Without these stalwarts of the game there could be no lucrative advertising contracts, book deals or headlines for the comparatively few 'stars'. All county cricketers have their moments of high achievement, of course, but in the eyes of the public they mainly form a supporting company for the small minority of box-office favourites. The great majority of players only reach the first-class game after a determined struggle; they find the financial rewards barely adequate (at least until recently), and they finish their careers with a continual awareness of the annual 'not re-engaged' list. These players, though, are the backbone on which the professional game is built.

As an example of the 'average' professional we will describe in more detail the career of Geoffrey Edrich, a Lancashire player from 1946 to 1958. His story is not highlighted because it is typical or indeed average – in fact, it is just the opposite – but because it raises many of the issues and events which impacted the careers of players in the immediate post-war era. A casual glance at *Wisden* might indicate that Edrich's cricket performances, while solid and dependable, lacked the high points achieved by a Denis Compton or Freddie Trueman. While this is true, Edrich's story (as told in Ralph Barker's excellent biography of the entire Edrich family) is a fascinating one and sheds much light on the influences of his time.

In cricket history Geoff Edrich will always be in the shadow of his elder brother Bill. In fact, there were four brothers who all played county cricket in the post-war years, the others being Eric (Lancashire) and Brian (Kent and Glamorgan).

Geoffrey's start in life was given an early setback when, due to the economic necessities of the early thirties, he was forced to leave school at the age of fourteen and to start work on his father's farm. There was, of course, a whole generation brought up in the depression years and, while this abrupt stop to education brought obvious disadvantages, for a person with the character associated with all the Edrich family it only increased the determination to become a professional cricketer. While the analogy of 'the best boxers are the hungry boxers' cannot be taken too far, it is not unreasonable to conclude that the career of professional cricketer held more appeal to a post-depression youth with no trade or qualifications than it would to someone with the present pre-ordained opportunity for 'A' levels and college. Until the improvements in education opportunities which came in the fifties, many future cricketers left school at fourteen and embarked on some type of manual labour or apprenticeship before becoming cricketers. Hence, the popular story of so many fast bowlers starting life as mine workers. With the rise of secondary and further education, however, this potential source of professional cricketers was seriously curtailed.

By the age of twenty-one Edrich had indeed put this setback behind him and had become a professional cricketer, albeit with the minor county of his birth, Norfolk. Here, his performances were sufficiently promising for him soon to attract the offer of a full contract with Hampshire. It seemed that the greatest opportunity of his life had arrived. Unfortunately, this coincided with the outbreak of the war, and young men like Edrich suddenly had far more important things to think about than cricket, or even careers.

When one reads of wartime charity cricket matches at Lord's, of 'Tests' in Egypt, of Compton scoring hundreds in India in 1944 it is tempting to think of cricketers as a separate, privileged breed during these war years. The truth, of course, was very far from this. There were many, like Keith Miller, who fought with great bravery; many, like Verity and Farnes, who lost their lives. Among the least fortunate, though, were those cricketers – Len Muncer, Ben Barnett, Laddie Outschoorn, E. W. Swanton and Geoff Edrich were the most famous – who became prisoners of the Japanese in the jungles of Burma and Siam.

In 1942 Edrich was listed as missing, presumed dead, and his young wife and newborn child received a widow's pension for two years before they learnt that he was, in fact, a POW working on the notorious Thailand railway. Somehow he survived the unbelievably harsh conditions but was not released until November 1945. Throughout that joyous summer of Victory Tests and celebration, Edrich was still in captivity. When he did finally return to England he was, of course, a changed man. His character, like that of all his contemporaries, was permanently marked. Strengthened in many ways, weakened in others, but above all he was now twenty-seven years old with no job, no training and a family to support. His only marketable talent – playing cricket – had lain dormant for the six most valuable years of a young player's development.

Resisting the temptation to give up all hopes of a cricket career, Geoffrey and his elder brother Eric approached several counties before eventually receiving contracts with Lancashire for the 1946 season. The Special Registration Rule, instituted in 1939, meant that they could play for an adopted county without a qualification period. Indeed, it was only through this rule that several counties were able to field sides of even moderate first-class standard in the first full post-war season. Edrich's salary for this first season was not high – at £313 it was less than that of a first-class umpire – but in his case it was supplemented by a 25% Army disability pension! Hardly the most propitious circumstances to attempt breaking into professional sport at such a mature age, but the pleasure in just being given the opportunity can well be imagined. Without wishing to sound sanctimonious, the comparison with the easier paths of today's young cricketers is somewhat striking.

No doubt the debilitating effects of survival in the jungle, combined with the strict food rationing imposed on post-war Britain, had an adverse effect but this was outweighed by the relief and delight at being home and playing cricket again. Luckily, the standard of county cricket was not high in those first few years and Edrich soon made his mark as a number three batsman and specialist close catcher. For the eleven seasons after cricket's resumption he was a valuable and regular member of a strong Lancashire team which contained a host of Test players. The closest Edrich came to representative honours was a tour to India with a strong Commonwealth team but playing county cricket was its own reward, his brothers were regular teammates and opponents on the circuit and he developed a keen interest in coaching the younger professionals.

Year in, year out Edrich could be relied on to score his share of runs – often when they were most needed – and in due course he was rewarded with a benefit in 1955. The importance and uncertainty of this most unsatisfactory of methods for rewarding a valued employee is well demonstrated in Edrich's case. In a good year the tax-free total from a benefit could be significant for the fortunate few. A major county such as Lancashire had produced figures as high as the £14,000 donated to Washbrook, but Geoffrey Edrich was less fortunate. An all-too-common combination of misfortunes resulted in only £3575 for the beneficiary, the lowest Lancashire total since the war.

Nevertheless, the next few years augured well for Edrich's future career. A spell as Lancashire captain in 1956 was greeted by critics and players as a great success. Washbrook was the regular captain but many felt that Edrich would make a good successor. In fact, the committee opted for a return to amateur captaincy and chose the inexperienced but highly promising Cambridge blue, Bob Barber. This did not really bother Edrich, however, as he intended his real future to lie in coaching and he was duly appointed 2nd XI captain and assistant club coach, a post he fulfilled successfully for two years.

The summer of 1959 was memorable for its weather and its cricket but for Geoff Edrich it brought disappointment and depression that bordered on the suicidal. In the middle of the season after the most trivial of high spirited incidents involving some of the young 2nd XI players, the faithful and effective club servant of thirteen years' standing was cruelly dismissed by the committee. Edrich's explanation runs as follows:

> I suppose there was a bit of jealousy at this time as quite a lot of the younger players always came to me for advice rather than the coach [Stan Worthington] and Washbrook. So when trouble came along in 1959 these two helped to push me out.
>
> You expect harsh treatment from the Japs: as I had during

my 3½ years POW in the Far East, but you don't expect it from Britishers on the Lancashire committee. I will never forgive them for the way they upset my wife and family.

It is all too easy to criticize cricket administrators, and county committees in particular. In truth, the vast majority of these people are among cricket's most valuable servants and passionately seek to improve and maintain the welfare of their clubs. Doubtless many of the apparently foolish decisions made by committees would appear fully justified if the public held possession of the full facts. Nevertheless, as noted in the previous chapter the post-war period produced some pretty curious decisions and the brutal and apparently thoughtless dismissal of Edrich was undoubtedly one of these. Happily, he eventually found a coaching appointment at Cheltenham College (through the help of Geoffrey Howard, then the Lancashire secretary) but, as he says, the memory of his leaving has lingered on.

Hardly a typical story it is true, but there were many others who crossed the same path at various points whether it be the lost war years, the failed benefit, the premature dismissal or the personality clash with captain or coach. Most of all, though, the likes of Geoffrey Edrich are best remembered as the backbone of English cricket – the solid, unspectacular county pro.

As the fifties and the sixties rolled by, this classic picture of the county cricketer, so often and faithfully described in John Arlott's books, began to change. The modern professional emerged and he certainly reflected modern society. He was more career and money conscious, perhaps better educated, more independent, and some would say less enamoured of the traditional values and virtues of his profession. This is not meant to be a criticism, but simply states that the modern cricketer, in keeping with his times, has a more realistic view of priorities and is less likely to play simply for 'the love of the game'. Some people have maintained that cricketers today are less diligent in their dedication to the game. Bob Taylor stated after the England tour of 1983/4 that some of his younger colleagues, 'seem much less conscientious about their game these days . . . the entire approach of many of them is less professional than it used to be . . . they have grown up in a different age and standards have changed, but it is my personal view that they haven't changed for the better.' While there does seem to be a lot of emphasis on non-cricket activities during tours these days, one should not forget the hard physical training that today's players often undertake, and the twelve-month-a-year playing schedule. Players of the early fifties were certainly not in such good physical condition as those of today, and it would be a harsh generalization to say that modern players do not work as hard at the game as did their predecessors.

Recently, there has been a significant increase in the number of professional cricketers who have graduated from the redbrick universities. Whether this is related to decreased employment opportunities elsewhere or the improved financial rewards now available to cricketers is arguable, but its effects are surely beneficial. Players such as Stovold, Rose, Allott, Hayes and many others are a cricketing resource that would probably have been lost thirty years ago. Similarly Oxbridge graduates like Marks, Roebuck, Tavare and Pringle are more likely to take up cricket as a profession than were their predecessors. Financially, a good case can now be made for entering cricket rather than joining the competition for conventional careers. During the fifties Frank Tyson was in many ways a forerunner of these modern, articulate players and his career, like Edrich's, is worthy of closer study.

Tyson, an English literature graduate and later a schoolmaster, hardly fits the traditional mould from which tearaway fast bowlers are made. Cricket writers of the romantic school would far rather that the 'Typhoon' (as he was so appropriately dubbed) had hailed from the coal mines like Larwood and Trueman, but he did not fit this stereotype and is, therefore, of interest to this book. While it is true that there were a few other county cricketers of the fifties who had attended redbrick universities – R. H. Maudsley, C. H. Palmer and G. G. Tordoff were prominent – they generally played as amateurs.

Tyson came from the respectable working-class surroundings of a council house in Middleton, near Manchester. His father, a foreman in the bleaching industry, always encouraged Frank's education above everything and he proved a successful student at the local grammar school. At the same time he showed above average cricket ability, playing in the tough atmosphere of the Central Lancashire League from the age of fifteen. Offered the chance of a contract with Lancashire at seventeen his father insisted on his going on to university instead. At that time, for a student like Tyson, university admission was considerably easier after some military service so begrudgingly a year was spent in the Army. His cricket hardly suffered since he played seven days a week for various teams. After leaving the Army he was admitted to Durham University to read English. The financial side of this move was made difficult by the death of his father, but Tyson found a novel way of paying his way through college – he became a professional cricketer, with Knypersley in the North Stafford-shire League. Spending every weekend of the summer term travelling from Durham to Stoke was not conventional under-graduate behaviour and had the inevitable result in failed exams. In fact, he was still studying for re-sits during the 1954/5 tour to Australia. It was this necessity, however, which started Tyson on his future path as a professional rather than amateur cricketer.

It was during his university career that Tyson was rejected by Lancashire and finally signed by Northamptonshire. Despite the fact that he was not wanted by the county of his birth he still had to serve a year's qualification for his adopted county since under the new rule they were only allowed a limited number of Special Registrations.

Tyson's meteoric rise to the top in cricket is well-known. Picked for the Australian tour after his first full county season (1954) his fast bowling dramatically and unexpectedly reached a peak which was only occasionally sustained after that one series. He remained a good fast bowler but not a superhuman one. This process was certainly accelerated by the strategy employed by Northants and other counties for wicket preparation in the mid-fifties. Every county had at least two good spinners and those at Northants (the Australians Tribe and Manning) were very good. As a consequence the groundsman was regularly ordered to scrape off the grass at the point just on a slow bowler's length. This resulted in a strip of peculiarly piebald appearance but, despite all the high principled directives periodically issued from Lord's for fast wickets, never brought any official censure.

Tyson's position as a professional cricketer who was also a university graduate made him a perceptive observer of the increasingly untenable situation of amateurs in cricket. One can well imagine his feelings on being censured by Freddie Brown during the 1958/9 tour to Australia for on one occasion publicly addressing the captain, Peter May, by his Christian name. May was a friend and fellow-university graduate, but in the con-ventions of cricket at that time he could not be addressed as 'Peter' by a professional such as Tyson. In the atmosphere of pre-war England, professionals such as Jack Hobbs or Wilfred Rhodes would never have questioned why they could not use the captain's first name, but in the different world of 1958, one can readily understand a trained, questioning mind like Tyson's finding the incident somewhat distasteful and symbolic of the anachronistic side of cricket. That the amateurs also found the situation absurd is demonstrated by the following story told by Rev. David Sheppard:

> When I was at Cambridge we played against Gloucestershire at Bristol. I made some runs, and, as we came off the field, Tom Graveney with whom I had made friends in 2nd XI matches said, 'Well played, David.' A few minutes later the Gloucestershire captain for that match walked into our dressing-room and came over to me. 'I'm terribly sorry about Graveney's impertinence,' he said. 'I think you'll find it won't happen again.' I found Tom as soon as I could, and said how sorry I was, and we have laughed about it often since.

Tyson's sensitivity to this amateur/professional topic is brought out in his own autobiography where he has some fairly harsh things to say about the issue, some of which have already been quoted in Chapter 5. Talking of the trouble-filled 1958/9 tour to Australia he refers to the 'rift between management and the ordinary rank-and-file', and the fact that there was 'little sympathy between amateurs and professionals'. The opinions of other professionals, however, would suggest that Tyson's views were in the minority. While there was frustration with a leaky and out-dated convention, there is little evidence for any personal animosity.

Tyson, then, was one example of the modern, graduate cricketer. He has been followed by many others and with their increased education level and career-awareness, a number of controversial issues have been brought to the surface. One which has already been touched on with respect to the Tom Graveney case is that of transferring from one county to another. This has always been repugnant to cricket administrators, who have continually warned against the evils of a soccer-style transfer market. Just recently, especially with the advent of high-priced overseas stars, a few cracks in the system have begun to appear. It was really in the fifties, however, that the harsh restrictions on such movements were first seriously challenged.

We have seen how the Special Registration Rule was instrumental in enabling some of the weaker counties to field competitive teams in the early post-war years. Whereas relatively few players changed counties before the war, most years in the fifties saw at least six or seven switches. The leading recipients were Northamptonshire, Somerset and Leicestershire, and the leading donor was Yorkshire. These players were mainly those who were unable to command a first-team place in the county of their birth, and so no objection could be found. Some were notable cricketers, however, including England players such as F. R. Brown, W. Watson, C. H. Palmer and R. Subba Row. Bob Berry, who was capped in 1950, even played for three different counties.

The trouble began when a few players decided to move despite still being required by their original county clubs. The issue was further complicated when the player concerned was an amateur and therefore, supposedly, not a paid employee of the club. In 1956 M. J. K. Smith who had played with success for his native Leicestershire during school and university holidays, decided to join Warwickshire as an amateur. Whatever the reason was, the Board of Control decided that the request for Special Registration could not be granted and Smith had to serve a one-year qualification for his new county.

In 1959 an even more prominent amateur cricketer was involved. Peter Richardson, the Worcestershire captain and highly successful England opening batsman, wrote to the county committee during his return voyage from the 1958/9 MCC tour to Australia. He simply stated that he no longer wished to play for the county and the reason was not disclosed to the press. Although an amateur, Richardson was dependent on his nominal post of secretary at Worcestershire for income. As soon as the rift was announced, offers for Richardson's services came in from several other counties and he stated that he would be happy to talk with them all as he had no predetermined preference. Worcestershire clearly did not wish to lose his valuable services and they tried everything to make him stay. It was announced that, 'Richardson was made aware that he would suffer no financial loss by remaining with Worcestershire as an amateur.' This somewhat startling statement clearly interested the MCC committee on amateur status and in May they formally asked Worcestershire to provide details of the agreement they had with Richardson as secretary to the club. By the end of the month, however, this had become somewhat academic as Richardson was released by Worcestershire and signed for Kent. Initially, Kent were undecided as to what his status would be but, after a meeting of their finance committee, it was announced that he would play as a professional, thereby providing a rare example of such a switch and reflecting the changing attitude towards shamateurism. Saving face was becoming less important and Richardson bravely chose the more honest approach. Worcestershire were somewhat embittered and refused to allow special registration. This meant that Richardson was out of cricket for a year, which coming on the top of his poor tour of Australia, severely hampered what had been a highly successful international career. He played happily on for Kent, though, and finally settled to farming in that county.

This controversial cricket transfer was soon to be followed by the Graveney affair, already discussed, which also resulted in a twelve-month qualification period. In 1962, however, the rules were amended to allow an amateur to change county without qualification provided he had 'adequate' reasons. This had come about partly as a result of the case involving Roger Prideaux. In January 1961 the twenty-two-year-old Kent batsman, then on a minor MCC tour in New Zealand, announced his desire to leave the county and join Somerset. After considerable success for Cambridge in 1960, Prideaux had found runs difficult to score in the county championship. Kent had a surfeit of openers – Richardson, Phebey and Wilson – and his place in the team became insecure; Prideaux felt a move to Somerset might assure him of a regular opener's spot. After talks with the club officials, however, he announced, 'I shall be pleased to stay with Kent. Obviously I would prefer to open the innings as I have had considerably more success there than lower down the order but I will be happy to leave the decision to the captain.'

In August the issue came to a head again when Prideaux was dropped after he preferred to play in a Scarborough Festival game rather than appear in a Championship match. The chance to join Northamptonshire as amateur player and assistant secretary was immediately accepted and the inevitable parting finally occurred. This was considered an adequate reason for transferring and no qualifying period was required, although from this distance it is hard to see a significant difference between this and Graveney's dispute with Gloucestershire.

Since that time there have been a number of other disputed transfers including Bob Willis, who had to miss half a season qualifying for Warwickshire. The question has become more and more clouded with the modern emphasis on the rights of an individual to ply his trade and the authorities have to tread more carefully in issuing twelve-month bans. This is very much in line with the moves in other sports and, indeed, in industry at large. Whilst it will be fought to the bitter end, the days of a true transfer system, or of players changing clubs at the end of each contract period, may not be so very far away.

This chapter has been necessarily brief and obviously could not do full justice to describing the post-war development of the professional cricketer, a subject which deserves a separate book. The better autobiographies can provide a good source for individual careers and, hopefully, at least some of the broader trends have been highlighted here. Certainly it is true that a tremendous change has occurred in the life of the county professional compared to the immediate post-war years. The type of person playing cricket has also changed. One retired cricketer commented on the changes with some regret:

> After the match we used to have a ball; go out and have a few beers and get back at three or four in the morning. The young player today comes off the field, takes a shower, has a meal, watches TV and goes to bed.

8

The Overseas Invasion

The presence of so many overseas players in English county cricket is often cited as a cause for the paucity of home-grown talent, particularly among fast bowlers. Recent legislation has sought to restrict the numbers of overseas players and the question has been further complicated by the qualification of a number of South Africans and West Indians to play for England. The historical background to this present situation is both interesting and instructive. It yet again shows that the key changes in attitude and action over this issue occurred in the early post-war era, and that they were linked to events outside the direct world of cricket.

Broadly speaking, there had been very few overseas players appearing in domestic English cricket before the second war. In many ways this scarcity helped to stimulate interest in the doings of a touring team. Especially in a world without television the foreign players had a genuine mystique that is largely missing today. Discounting the essentially English players who simply happened to be born overseas, such as P. F. Warner, and those who adopted England at an early age, like Sammy Woods, there had been a few genuine imports who added spice and variety to the county programme.

The earliest examples were, naturally enough, Australians. What is perhaps more surprising is that two of the earliest immigrants were the finest bowler and batsman Australia had produced until that time – Frank 'The Demon' Spofforth and Billy Murdoch. Both played in England as amateurs after their careers in Australia were over but, in their mid-thirties, they were able to make a significant contribution to their respective counties, Derbyshire and Sussex. Spofforth, it is true, did not play a great deal for Derbyshire (1889-91), who anyway were rated as a second-class county at that time, but he subsequently enlivened many post-season festival games. He topped the national averages in 1896 (aged forty-three) and continued to play for Hampstead well into old age. Essentially, though, he was a businessman (he became Managing Director of the Star Tea Company) who played a little cricket when convenient. Murdoch was somewhat different in that he came to England after the 1890 Australian tour, principally to play cricket. Considered too old at thirty-six by some in Australia, he proceeded to enjoy many more years with Sussex, whom he captained from 1893 to 1899, and with London County. In addition to this pair, J. J. Ferris also played three seasons for Gloucestershire after the 1890 Australian tour.

Murdoch, in particular, became a colourful part of the English cricket scene during the nineties and was followed by more Australians. They were few in number compared to the post-war era but they were high in quality. The chief recipient was Middlesex, a county which perhaps due to its London location and Lord's tradition has always had a cosmopolitan flavour. Throughout the nineties Jim Phillips, more famous now as an umpire, had played for the county. Phillips was years ahead of his time in the way he would play or umpire in big cricket all through the year, virtually commuting between Australia and England. More important from a playing point of view was Middlesex's recruitment in 1896, through Phillips' recommendation, of the outstanding young Australian all-rounder, Albert Trott. He was followed in 1903 by Frank Tarrant. After serving their two-year qualification periods, both made outstanding contributions to English cricket. Trott may have been the more attractive and his fame has certainly survived the passing years, but Tarrant was the more effective cricketer and statistically was one of the leading all-rounders of the Golden Age.

A few other Australians followed the examples of these great players but, talented though they were, none of them played long enough to make a major impact. The two-year qualifying period was a big deterrent and a special reason (like Trott's grudge against omission by the selectors) was needed. In the period up to 1914 there were three other notable foreigners who adorned the county game, none of them Australian. These were C. B. Llewellyn, a South African who played for Hampshire, C. A. Ollivierre of Derbyshire, the first West Indian to qualify for a county, and the legendary K. S. Ranjitsinhji of Sussex. Ranji, of course, lent a mystical sparkle to the Golden Age that personifies that era in the minds of cricket-lovers. Like several of the other imports he went on to represent England in Test Matches. Messrs Lamb and Smith of the 1983 team are, therefore, only following in the ancient footsteps of Murdoch, Trott and Ranji as 'non-English' Englishmen.

Between the wars there were still very few overseas players willing to pay the price of a two-year qualification for county cricket. The majority of those that did were, like most of their predecessors, amateurs; this, despite the improving financial position of the English professional of those times. Apart from one notable Australian, the great fast bowler E. A. Macdonald of Lancashire, the main Antipodean imports were from New Zealand, by then a Test playing country. No less than five members of their first touring team to England (1927) played county cricket at one time or another. The most accomplished was undoubtedly Stewart Dempster, who took up a business appointment with Sir Julien Cahn while qualifying for Leicestershire. The others, Tom Lowry (Somerset), C. C. R. Dacre (Gloucestershire), Ken James and Bill Merritt (both Northamptonshire) also brought a high degree of skill and entertainment value to the county game.

The situation after the Second World War could not have been more different. The counties were desperately short of talented players and nobody minded if a few overseas players could be used to fill the gaps. The strict qualification rule of two years' residence was not always tightly enforced in those first few post-war years, but this seemed appropriate in the short term. In conjunction with the Special Registration Rule enabling inter-county transfers, it enabled the weaker counties to at least field a competitive team.

The most numerous influx of players during the late forties and early fifties came from Australia. The initial attraction, however, was not county cricket but the northern leagues, particularly in Lancashire. During the twenties, the league professional had gradually changed from being a club servant to a highly paid, competitively recruited overseas star. Ted Macdonald, Learie Constantine and George Headley led the way, and the trend accelerated after the war. All the great names took their turn in the leagues – Lindwall, Worrell, Weekes, Walcott, Ramadhin, Mankad, and, later, Gilchrist, Hall, Sobers and a host of others. The reasons were simply economic; there was scarcely any opportunity to become a professional cricketer in the West Indies or Australia, so unless one had a very lucrative non-cricket job why not make £1000 or so for four or five months' work and then return to the domestic season? While this was true for the top stars mentioned, it seemed that many of the Australians who came to the leagues did not want to return for a winter in Sheffield Shield cricket. Some were simply not top-class players, others had grudges against the selection procedure in Australia, and some had grown accustomed to England during their war service here. The universally friendly attitude towards a league pro in Lancashire also had its effect.

By the early fifties, a number of these Australian league players drifted into county cricket – again for a variety of reasons. Although the two-year qualification still existed, a player's league commitments were often not interrupted and the challenge of a higher standard of cricket must have been great. Also the desire to show the Australian selectors what they were missing surely must have motivated some. This pattern of a few years in the leagues followed by a county career was followed by Dooland (Notts), Tribe and Livingston (both Northants), Grieves (Lancs), Pettiford (Kent) and Alley (Somerset). Other Australians arrived via variations on this theme – Manning (Northants), Walker (Notts), McMahon (Surrey, Somerset), Dollery (Warwicks) and McCool (Somerset). As well as those well-known names, there were quite a number of young Australians who tried their hand in England without quite making the grade. Also, some never left the leagues. The best example here is Cec Pepper, the legendary all-rounder who later became a first-class umpire. The stories of Pepper's volatile and entertaining character even outweigh those of his record-breaking performances on the field. All in all, there must have been quite a camaraderie amongst the ex-patriot Aussies during the early fifties, particularly in Lancashire. We should also not forget the continued presence of two notable all-rounders who had started their county careers before the war – Jack Walsh and Vic Jackson of Leicestershire. Recruited by Sir Julien Cahn before hostilities began, they started their county careers in earnest in 1946 and more or less carried the Leicestershire team for a number of years. In this respect their pedigree was similar to that of Stewart Dempster. Cahn, incidentally, also brought over two other Australian players who had narrowly missed selection for the 1938 tour, Harold Mudge and Ginty Lush; they would probably have qualified for Leicestershire but for the outbreak of war.

This glut of Australians were not, however, the only overseas players recruited by the counties during the fifties. There is a long list of South Africans, Indians, West Indians, Pakistanis and New Zealanders who also appeared, but the unfortunate feature is that most of them were, at best, only average performers. Certainly they were able to hold a place in the generally weak county sides of the immediate post-war period, but they did not bring the extra skill and panache that would justify the exclusion of a young English player. The counties which relied the heaviest on such players were Northants, Leicestershire, Nottingham-shire, Somerset and Warwickshire. Warwickshire showed the success of such an approach by carrying off the championship in 1951 with virtually no 'star' players. Their team included Hitchcock, Don Taylor, Pritchard (all New Zealanders) and K. Dollery (Australian). In addition, at least half a dozen other overseas players were given a trial by the county during the fifties.

Just as successful was the policy of Northamptonshire, who were bolstered by a thriving supporters' club and the sponsorship of British Timken Ltd. As well as providing the incentive for English-born players, such as Freddie Brown, to move from other counties, Timken provided off-the-field jobs for George Tribe, Jock Livingston, John Manning (all Australian) and Peter Arnold (New Zealand). Their presence in the fifties really dragged Northants from being a Cinderella county to one challenging for the championship. The policy was not a short-sighted one, as money was applied to a local youth policy. Who is to say that the crop of attractive young players produced in the late seventies were not directly products of that scheme?

As we have said, there were many 'journeyman' overseas players in county cricket during the fifties. Perhaps the only 'star' who has not been mentioned was the West Indian Roy Marshall of Hampshire. Unlike today, however, these players gave up the opportunity to play Test Cricket once they threw in their lot with a county. A player such as Marshall would have broken his English county qualification if he had played Test cricket for his country in the off-season. In 1951 Alf Valentine agreed to join Worcestershire but changed his mind on discovering his inter-national career would be over. This rule, which appears rather harsh in today's atmosphere of court actions for 'restraint of trade', was not changed until 1962. Even then such a player was barred from appearing for his native country on a tour to England. Of course, the other side of the coin was the possibility of quali-fying to play for England. Four years' residence was needed and certainly Marshall's case was discussed in this context. On strictly playing merit it is hard to see why he was not included at some stage in the late fifties or early sixties. There had been precedents for foreigners playing Test cricket for England in the shape of the three notable Indians – Ranji, his nephew Duleep and the Nawab of Pataudi (four Australians – Ferris, Murdoch, Trott and Woods – also played but only in matches against South Africa which were not regarded as 'true' Tests at the time). These three Indians, however, were not only amateurs and old blues but also of noble birth in India. Somehow this was acceptable whereas the humble Barbadian, Marshall, was not. This hesitation was subsequently waived in the case of Basil d'Oliveira (Test debut 1966) and Tony Greig (1970), both South Africans. By this time, public opinion and that of the game's administrators had changed sufficiently for both players to be generally welcomed. More recently the cases of Lamb and Smith have opened the controversy again. It is hard to see where a strict policy is drawn since Mike Procter was not chosen when qualified, yet clearly had strong claims on merit.

The question of qualification period is one that has brought heated debate ever since that first influx of foreign talent after the war. In the early post-war years the normal requirement was two years' continuous residence in the county and many players duly fulfilled this. An exception, however, was made for any overseas cricketer who had not played for his own State or Province side during the previous two years. In these cases a period of only one year's residence was needed in the county. Many of the Australians playing in the leagues fell into this category so the switch to a county like Northamptonshire only required a single year's residence.

By 1951 this easing of the rule was causing some concern and the ACCC decided to increase the qualification period to a full three years in all cases, with no cricket contract to be undertaken outside the county. The new rule was not enforced until 1954 after which it had the effect that very few established cricketers, like Dooland or Tribe, were prepared to sit out three years in minor cricket and be unable to take on a league engagement. 'The added year may well lead to the eventual disappearance of the overseas player from English county cricket, for very few counties would be prepared to pay and wait for three years for a new man,' was the *Cricketer*'s judgement. While the goal of developing young English-born cricketers was clearly a worthy one, the following years, as we have seen, brought nothing but decay and decline in the viability of the game. The turning-point in the question of overseas players was reached as an aftermath of the 1960/61 West Indian tour to Australia. The public's imagination was so caught by the tourists that the three biggest names – Kanhai, Sobers and Hall – were offered immediate qualification to play for State sides in the Sheffield Shield. The effect on the following domestic season of 1961/62 was nothing short of devastating. Ray Robinson, the veteran Australian journalist, wrote:

> That persistent clanking you hear in the background comes from turnstiles as Australia's inter-state cricket makes a comeback as a Spectator Sport as crowds have thickened for at least two good reasons. Besides being a reminder of past excitements, the presence of three West Indian guest artists added spice to the season . . . Richie Benaud's policies have inspired other State captains to show similar enterprise . . . The MCC in October will begin play in a country expecting action-packed cricket at all times . . . Play chock full of incident stimulated the liveliest interest in Sheffield Shield cricket since pre-war days . . . Most matches ended with boys rushing the ground to escort their heroes to the pavilion.

One can well imagine the English county secretaries, their own finances in tatters, drooling at the possibility of a similar turnaround in this country. At the spring meeting of the ACCC the idea of immediate registration of 'star' players was indeed discussed but met with little support because of the fear that poorer counties would not be able to compete. Instead, the somewhat lukewarm compromise of reducing the qualification period back from three years to two was passed. The attraction of this instant remedy for falling gates could not be resisted for long, however, and once the plunge had been successfully taken for the Gillette Cup, the inevitable finally occurred in time for the 1968 season. Then, for the first time, English county cricket was able to embrace the true Test Match 'stars' of other countries. In that first season of 1968 the spectators were able to feast on the likes of Sobers, Kanhai, Lloyd and Gibbs from the West Indies; Procter and Barry Richards from South Africa; Asif from Pakistan, Engineer from India, Turner from New Zealand and Greg Chappell from Australia. This marvellous cross-section of talents was supplemented the following summer by McKenzie and Intikhab. The players were successful and the game certainly benefited as if from a blood transfusion. The timing was right as it never would have been before by virtue of the presence of the one-day competitions. These imported players were made for such cricket. In addition, 1968 saw the introduction of first-innings' bonus points and a strong move to improve the quality of pitches: both factors helped display the talents of these players to the full.

Since then, of course, the situation has got rather out of hand. If the counties had stuck to just one star quality player each, then the novelty and stimulating effect could have been sustained. It was the gradual inclusion of the 'average' overseas player – similar to the early fifties situation – that eroded the beneficial effect, until, in the eighties, the administrators are struggling to back-track and restrict the flow. The problem stemmed from the fact that these immediately registered cricketers became 'English' for the purposes of county cricket after five years. This enabled a nucleus of overseas players to be built up by some counties. Despite the efforts to restrict each county to one player not qualified for England, the situation is becoming absurd. At the beginning of the 1984 season the following overseas *fast bowlers* were contracted to counties:

Derbyshire	— Holding	Middlesex	— Daniel
	Mortenson	Northamptonshire	— Hanley
Essex	— Phillip	Nottinghamshire	— Hadlee
Glamorgan	— Davis		Rice
Gloucestershire	— Walsh	Somerset	— Garner
Hampshire	— Marshall	Surrey	— Clarke
	Small, M.	Sussex	— Imran Khan
	Reifer		Le Roux
Kent	— Baptiste	Warwickshire	— Small, G.
	Alderman	Worcestershire	— Ellcock
Lancashire	— Jefferies		Kapil Dev
Leicestershire	— Carmichael		
	Roberts		
	Clift		
	Ferris		

Not all these can play at once, of course, which makes the situation even more ridiculous. In the spring of 1984 the counties had been thrown into confusion by the forthcoming West Indian tour in which at least six fast bowlers were expected to be included. There was an unseemly rush to obtain replacements which at times bordered on the farcical. Gloucestershire went to great pains to secure the signature of Courtney Walsh only to find him a surprise selection for the tour. Hampshire signed Milton Small as cover for Malcolm Marshall only to seen him become a Test Match player, necessitating the arrival of Elvis Reifer as double cover. Never a thought, of course, of relying on home-grown talent.

Another trend which has brought an increased overseas flavour to county cricket is the presence of West Indians and Asians who were born in Britain or immigrated at an early age. Some of these, like Gordon Greenidge, have opted for their country of birth, but most are now English by nationality and Test Match allegiance. The trend is even more pronounced in the world of football, and in both sports these players are beginning to attain English international honours. The presence of these players is another example of cricket being dependent on social history. Between 1946 and 1964 there were three-quarters of a million Common-wealth immigrants to Britain; by 1963 there were more than a quarter of a million West Indians alone on these shores. It is, therefore, hardly surprising that talented footballers and cricketers should be emerging from these immigrant families by the 1980s. They are more likely to be found playing for counties near the centre of immigrant population, so it is not surprising that Middlesex open the bowling with Cowans and Williams while Slack and Butcher appear as batsmen. These players are bringing a fine variety to the county circuit with Asif Din, Dipak Patel, Damian d'Oliveira and Nasir Zaidi showing that one does not have to be of West Indian descent to succeed.

It is sad to relate that, in some cases, these players are having their fully justified presence in county cricket questioned because of the overabundance of the artificially imported overseas stars. The balance will have to be restored soon if the England team is to remain competitive. Surely the counties will see sense or the near-term financial benefits of having West Indian fast bowlers will be offset by reduced TCCB profits as a result of a permanently weak international team.

9
Up-to-Date

Thus far, we have studied the connection between cricket and the continually evolving social and economic scene in Britain. In particular, it is apparent that while cricket has never been a static, unchanging game, it underwent perhaps its most dramatic alteration in character during the years 1946-1963. It is surely not coincidental that these were also years of major change in the everyday life and environment of the country as a whole. But what of the twenty years or so since 1963? Naturally enough that year was not a sharp dividing line, even though a number of momentous developments crystallized at once, both in the game and the broader sphere. The major themes that we have already discussed continued to evolve right through the sixties and seventies to the present day with only the emphasis changing, first one issue assuming centre stage, then another. It has long been a truism in cricket, as in life, that there is no 'new' development that has not been seen or foreseen at some point in history. It is amusing to read Anthony Trollope's visionary account of a Test Match in 1980 written more than a hundred years ago. The batsman wears 'a machine upon his head by which his brain and features are protected', and the fall of each wicket is greeted by 'a sound of kettle-drums, trumpets, fifes and clarinets, and a huge gun is let off'. The accuracy of these predictions is uncanny.

While we have tended to paint the revolution in cricket that occurred in the early sixties as being a panacea which rescued the game from its economic and stylistic death throes of the late fifties, the cynic could argue that the story of the last twenty years shows that a huge price was paid for that resuscitation. Some would claim that the game which charmed countless generations and reflected England's noblest virtues has sold its birthright for the lure of commercialism and greed. For those who have followed the preceding arguments in this book, however, this outraged cry of the traditionalists must be ignored. It has no more relevance than the pleas that traditionalists have always made over the last two hundred years or more. By now it is clear that cricket in general, in spite of the well-meaning contributions from administrators, has not the slightest choice in which direction its evolution lies. As an entertainment, pastime or occupation of the people it will simply follow modern attitudes and trends with unerring faithfulness. Cricket is not unique in this – all the major sports and pastimes have shared the same social driving forces over the recent past; they have suffered from similar problems and controversies, and benefited from related improvements and modernizations.

In bringing this story up to date, then, we can conveniently divide recent developments into two main categories. Firstly, the general characteristics of the game – its style and customs – and secondly, the behavioural or people-related aspects. In the former area, undoubtedly the most dominating feature has been the strength of the one-day game including both county and international competitions. The effects of this emphasis on limited-overs cricket are well-known. On the positive side there is the improved fielding, taking of quick singles, thoughtful captaincy, fast run-scoring, close finishes and a general feeling of urgency and fast tempo. The negative aspects include decline of the spinner, encouragement of negative tactics in the field and the falling-off in Test Match batting. As we have said, a price has been paid for the modernization of the game – only time will tell whether the price is too high.

There is another interesting aspect to this modern obsession with the one-day game. It fits a clear post-war trend in sport of greater and greater emphasis being placed on the result of a match rather than the attractiveness or quality of the entertainment being provided. This trend is most obviously apparent in football where the dullest of 1-0 victories will satisfy the majority of home fans. Cricket is in danger of following the same path. The one-day game encourages this, with its soccer-style Cup Finals and fervour. The attitude towards overseas players in county cricket further exemplifies it. While everyone agrees there are too many foreign stars and that English cricket suffers, the counties cannot bring themselves to enforce a serious reduction; instead they struggle to maximize their own squad of foreigners. If a touring team is due to claim an overseas star then a one-season replacement is sought. A reserve overseas man who cannot routinely play because of the limitation on numbers is kept on standby in the second eleven. This is all part of the win-at-all-costs attitude that has taken over. Not that this is wholly bad since surely keen competition is vital to the well-being of the game. There is a danger, however, of a deterioration in ethics or conduct and this is in accord with modern social trends. The ready-made solution, pre-packaged for instant use, appears to be the order of the day, with the end certainly justifying the means.

The emphasis on the result to the exclusion of style is not simply a symptom of one-day cricket. Test Matches, which have assumed overwhelming attention compared to other games, are played in the same atmosphere. As the number of Tests being played has expanded dramatically so their worth has been devalued. The Jet Age has enabled more tours to be squeezed into the itinerary but the real driving force is the fact that Tests bring large profits. While this is partly due to paying attendances, the key ingredients for one-day games and Tests are the sponsorship and television revenue they attract. We have traced the tentative beginnings of these two factors in early post-war cricket and their growth continued to be steady and significant during the sixties and seventies. It was the Packer crisis, however, that single-handedly pitched both into the driving seat as far as the running of the game is concerned. Now that the original hysterical reaction to Packer and World Series Cricket has subsided, a more balanced review of events can be made. The most obvious outcome is that the average county player as well as the Test star has received the increased rewards that were so long overdue – almost fatally overdue. The speed with which traditional cricket put its house in order in the face of Packer was almost unseemly. By 1978 the England touring fee had risen by 67% from the previous year, the Test Match fee for players had skyrocketed to £1000 and that for umpires had risen from a mere £175 to £750. Although the ordinary county player did not immediately benefit from Packer, the Players' Association was, in turn, able to negotiate much improved minimum salaries for county cricketers. All this money, of course, was found through sponsorship. During 1978 the following approximate amounts were received for the major competitions:

Company	Amount £
Cornhill Insurance	175,000
Schweppes	175,000
Benson and Hedges	130,000

John Player	130,000
Gillette	100,000
Prudential	250,000

In addition, Bonusbonds, Wrigley, Whitbreads, Wilkinson Sword, Holt Products and Commercial Union were all supporting events around the period 1978-79, although some had started earlier. The Test and County Cricket Board have recently been able to translate this large income into massive annual surpluses in excess of £1 million for distribution to the counties. The Ashes season of 1981 provided tremendous income and some counties reported profits in six figures. It is too early to say whether this was a temporary peak and to predict that the post-Packer honeymoon is now over but clearly there has been cause for concern as the 1980s progress. Cricket clubs, like their counterparts in football, are beginning to walk a tightrope of financial solvency yet again. Profits have turned into losses; the players may be higher paid but the size of many of the county staffs is being reduced. There is a continual battle to keep the all-important sponsors.

The seventies were really the 'boom' period for sponsorship of major sporting events. Cricket, if anything, was a little slow to take advantage of the trend (or be taken advantage of, depending on your view regarding the dangers of commercialism), the leading exponents being the motor sports. In addition, horse-racing, golf, soccer and tennis have all competed successfully for the sponsor's favour, and even the minority events such as yacht and powerboat races, cycling, snooker, darts, squash, etc., are typically associated with a newspaper, tobacco firm, oil company or insurance group. Another trend that gained ground in the seventies was the sponsorship of individual players rather than tournaments or clubs. Barry Richards was an early example with deals such as $1 per run from Coca Cola in Australia and four rand per run from an ice-cream merchant in Durban. In county cricket Sobers was reputedly paid £3000 per season by a group of local Northamptonshire businessmen and, more recently, Brian Davison was privately sponsored because Leicestershire would not meet his salary requirements. While there is a potential danger in that an individually sponsored player might play for his pocket rather than for the team, one can hardly complain at the performances of the players named. If they were ever batting purely to maximize the monetary reward it never showed.

Another modern trend in professional sport, and one which has been analysed rigorously by economists, is the deliberate establishment of so-called 'uncertainty of outcome'. The theory predicts that spectator interest, and therefore profits, will be maximized by close competition between as many teams as possible or 'equalization of success'. This idea is more clearly practised in the main American sports – football, baseball, ice hockey and basketball. The pooling of league income amongst member clubs is one method of achieving equality, but by far the most drastic is the way in which the players are allocated to a particular club. An annual 'draft' is conducted in which the finest college players are chosen by the professional clubs in a strict rotation. The teams select players in the reverse order that they finished the previous season's competition. This enables a Cinderella club to rebuild into a powerful team in only a few years. This strict control of the playing talent, having no regard to the player's birthplace or even his desires, has resulted in a tremendous increase in uncertainty of outcome whereby almost every team in the league has a chance of winning the competition.

Cricket has clearly moved in a similar direction, although by more subtle means. In terms of finance, the league income – international matches, sponsorship, TV income, etc. – is very definitely pooled via the TCCB share-out to the counties. All clubs profit from this, regardless of performance. Secondly, the allocation of playing talent has been more equitably shared not via a draft but by the introduction of 'instant' overseas stars. The 'uncertainty of outcome' has been further aided by the introduction of one-day competitions and the result is clear to see in the lists of competition winners over the last twenty years. The familiar names of Yorkshire, Surrey, Lancashire and the other big-name teams are now far more likely to be replaced by the one-time poor relations like Essex and Somerset. The Sunday League, which is cricket in its most truncated and artificial form, provides the most obvious example of this equalization of success.

Most people seem to agree that this added competitive element has been good for cricket and it has certainly stimulated interest in some of the smaller counties. Yet again, it is clear that cricket is simply obeying the same economic driving forces that dominate other sports and indeed any market economy. Where this will lead in the future is anybody's guess but it is not unreasonable to postulate further 'Americanization' of the sport. A draft system for the overseas players, whereby the counties choose in turn from an available pool, is not beyond the bounds of possibility. Indeed, we are getting closer every season as the West Indian fast bowlers jump from county to county depending on immediate expediency. Another classic feature of American sport, the end-of-season play-offs, could also become a reality in cricket, particularly in the ailing County Championship. Packer already used the idea in his World Series Cricket matches whereby a league system is only the preliminary means of selecting the teams for a final series of knock-out matches. Rugby League has gone this route and English cricket may not be far behind. It aims to keep the maximum number of teams in contention for honours and provides an end-of-season TV and spectator bonanza.

Switching now to the behavioural side of cricket during the last twenty years or so, we find ourselves in an area that has been filled with controversy and incident. In Chapter 6 it was clear that the first two post-war decades were characterized by an increase in conflict and argument much of which was linked to the incompatible attitudes of a rather old-fashioned and conservative administration or employer group and the emerging post-war culture which questioned the status quo. During the late sixties and through to the present, however, these flames have been fanned at times into an inferno. The controversies of the fifties seem somewhat tame in comparison with the sensations that have filled the ever-hungry headlines of Fleet Street. Here again, cricket has simply shared the spotlight with other professional sports.

A key notion in describing these modern events must be that in various ways they have reflected a struggle for power. Whether it has been Packer against the cricket establishment, rebel players against their home authorities, players fighting their county committees, the black nations opposing links with South Africa, or the struggle within the TCCB and MCC, the key ingredient has been one group trying to wrest the power from another. The analogy with broader social development goes without saying. The Packer Affair was the greatest cricket 'power play' of all time, and must surely illustrate some of the themes already mentioned. The facts are recent enough to be familiar to most cricket followers and have indeed been the subject of whole books – they will not be rehashed here. The reader is referred to the *Wisdens* of the period, *Barclays World of Cricket*, and the books by Blofeld, McFarlane and Caro. The two aspects that will be discussed here are firstly the reasons for the whole affair, and secondly the behaviour of cricket's ruling bodies.

Starting with the reasons, let us first of all say that it is not merely with hindsight that one can say the whole episode was inevitable. E. V. Lucas, writing before the war, made the following prediction:

> I have no doubt that a showman will, before long, rent a ground or a stadium and engage a team of sloggers to fill two hours, or even that he will arrange contests of tip and run. Let him. It will be good fun for the impatient; but it won't be cricket. It will be as like cricket as a music-hall programme is like a play by Shakespeare.

Mr Justice Slade, who heard the court case between Packer and the TCCB, rightly pointed out that a challenge from a private promoter was bound to come and he was surprised it had not happened before. Once again, it is instructive to look at the sporting scene in the USA. While many will argue that there is no similarity between baseball or American football and cricket, they are forgetting that the key factors in US professional sport are commercialism, sponsorship, profit and television. Since all these factors are increasingly dominating cricket, the same driving forces are now in place and one can expect similar repercussions no matter how fundamentally dissimilar the games. Basketball is very different in character from American football, but it exhibits the same problems and socio-economic developments — the pattern is repeated throughout the world, including Britain. Anyway, the point to be made is that it has been common in US sport for rival leagues or competitions to be set up by 'rebel' entrepreneurs in defiance of the existing established authorities. Even in the last few years a new football league (US Football League) has been formed and is causing all sorts of argument and friction with the established National Football League by enticing their star players. The result of these renegade leagues has, almost without exception, been their disappearance either through lack of success, or more often by being merged into the existing league. A compromise has always been found because the negotiating parties are always businessmen first and foremost. While cricket's 'amateur' administrators may have thought it impossible for a rival competition to be set up outside their aegis, any US sporting economic historian could have predicted it and also the inevitability of a compromise solution. He might also have saved the TCCB £250,000 in legal fees. Of course, British sports economists and sociologists understand this too. Peter Sloane has described the final agreement with Packer in the terms of the professional economist:

> Monopoly was restored to the product market. Yet the market may not be quite the same as before, since there will be more awareness of the threat of potential competition if the monopoly becomes too restrictive or fails to meet the changing tastes of consumers.

Even the original cause of the Packer intrusion – seeking of exclusive TV rights – need not be a surprise, and is not a unique occurrence. Even within British sport we have seen the related fuss caused by the Football League in 1978 when they attempted to grant London Weekend Television such an agreement. Again the affair went to the High Court before a solution was reached.

Let us turn now to the effect of the Packer initiative on the established ruling bodies of cricket – basically the TCCB, ACB and ICC. Initially, these people, in common with the majority of cricket enthusiasts, were blinded with rage at the actions of Packer and the players he contracted, particularly Tony Greig, the England captain, who acted as secret recruiting agent. While most of the game's administrators surely supported the political ideal of private enterprise they were appalled to meet it head on in the world of cricket. A 'holier than thou' attitude was taken with the players and the initial reaction was to ban them from all first-class and Test cricket. The players had been tempted by the lure of money and this was to be their punishment – it was almost the old master-servant relationship again with the master feeling betrayed. By 1977, however, the world had changed dramatically and the authorities made a fatal error in not recognizing it. While a hard line may have worked during the Nottinghamshire players' strike of 1881 it would not in the modern world. The TCCB found themselves in the High Court under charges of Restraint of Trade and inducement to breaches of contract. Even worse, the court case was won by the players in an overwhelming fashion, the Judge being quite adamant in his condemnation of cricket's ruling bodies and their dictatorial attempts to punish the players. In a way this defeat in court was a key point in the development of modern cricket. It cleared the way, rightly or wrongly, for a new era of commercialization of the game, and freedom of movement for the players, far more extreme than anything dreamt of in the fifties and sixties. In doing so, cricket was suddenly dragged into the mainstream of the modern sports industry. We have traced the early roots of this development in the fifties and sixties; Packer merely gave the natural evolution of the game a quantum leap. Within a couple of years cricket was in the forefront of the Americanization of British sport. It is not surprising that this conversion of cricket should be initiated in Australia where the way of life is generally more influenced by the USA than by the older, traditional ties with Britain. Yet again, cricket in Australia is faithfully reflecting life in Australia.

The balance between the beneficial and harmful aspects of this modern cricket revolution depend on one's personal bias, of course, but some conclusions can be made. Firstly, it is surely a desirable result that the Cricketers' Association are more involved in the decision-making process of modern cricket. This involve-ment had been occurring slowly but was given a tremendous boost by the terrible beating the authorities took at the hands of Packer. Stung by Mr Justice Slade's accusation of 'dictators' the TCCB now defer to the Association more and more on matters of policy. What remnants that still existed of 'them' and 'us' have been finally swept away. Secondly, the improved financial lot of cricketers cannot be begrudged. The old attitude was almost one of 'They have an enjoyable life and are not qualified for anything else so why should they complain about salary?'. This is gradually being replaced by a modern recognition of the leading players as entertainers at the top of their profession. Thirdly, one wholly undesirable development of the Packer affair has been direct involvement and even control by sponsors in the running of the game. This never occurred before and is a potential danger. Again, it is an almost inevitable step in the Americanization of cricket. Money, and especially television money, dictates the laws, style and structure of modern sport and cricket is moving swiftly to join the trend.

While the Packer affair was mainly involved with the struggle for power between the established rulers of the game and the commercial world of TV and sponsorship, an undercurrent of jockeying for power between players and administrators has continued. We have described the beginnings of this movement during the fifties when the players were usually on the losing side, just as they had been right back to the days of the Nottinghamshire Schism. Recently, however, the balance of power has shifted towards the players just as it has in other sports throughout the world. Freedom of movement from employer to employer has been the principal forum – indeed it was at the heart of the Packer affair as far as the players were concerned. In previous days the likes of Graveney and others typically lost their battle to change counties without restriction. In 1980, however, Barry Wood sought to leave Lancashire within forty-eight hours of banking a benefit cheque for £62,429. The TCCB, sharing the outrage of the average cricket fan, sought to ban the move to Derbyshire. Their decision to outlaw Wood until 30 July was hastily modified to 4 June after the threat of legal action. This whole case was symptomatic of the times and the TCCB treat such cases with kid gloves now that legal action is an ever-present recourse.

The move to unionize professional sportsmen occurred throughout the world during the sixties and cricket followed suit. In British soccer, of course, the Union is even more to the fore and in the late seventies freedom of contract was introduced (subject to a negotiated transfer fee). As more and more established cricketers – both domestic and imported – find reasons to want to change counties, this issue will monopolize more and more of the headlines in cricket. 'Player power' is not an issue that will go away. Indeed, the Yorkshire club's vicissitudes of recent years are a reflection, in part, of the tremendous power wielded by Geoffrey Boycott. There are some interesting parallels between this case and the Wardle affair of 1958. Both players were undoubtedly of great value on the playing side but supposedly had a negative influence on team building. In the case of Wardle the committee sacked him without any fear of contradiction. By 1983, when the same thing was tried on Boycott, in the same county, the response was to throw out the committee. Even the most revered names in the history of the county were not safe from the power Boycott and his followers wielded. As another example of so-called Player Power we have discussed the possibility of strikes by the players in Chapter 6. It is interesting that John Snow in his autobiography reports two instances in 1975 when this almost came to pass. On totally separate issues the players of Worcestershire and Lancashire almost refused to play for the county because they could not get a fair hearing from their employers. While things were eventually patched up, a certain amount of bitterness resulted and it is not clear who were the victors.

Leaving aside the quest for power, another aspect of modern cricket which concerns many lovers of the game is the increase in poor behaviour on the part of the players. This again is a symptom that cricket shares with most other professional sports. Fred Inglis, in his book *The Name of the Game*, lays the blame squarely on the presence of big money:

> The injection of all this money has caused the winning of games to be financially important; in these circumstances, the good loser naturally disappears. Tactics become fouler and fouler . . . the adjective 'professional', when it does not mean 'dull', means 'dirty'.

While this unpleasant trend is apparent in football and, to some extent, tennis, it is certainly not the case in golf where huge sums of money are at stake. Here, of course, there is no real opponent other than the golf course and a gentlemanly demeanour is usually maintained. Cricket falls in a crucial in-between category. At the professional level, particularly in Test Matches, the incidence of sharp or questionable tactics has been growing since the war. Even more alarming is the rise of bad-tempered and physically aggressive behaviour towards opponents and umpires, an altogether newer phenomenon. It is not so widespread yet that it cannot be checked but the move must be made soon. The Australian approach of judgement and fines being decided by fellow-players appears to be a sensible approach and is another step away from the dictatorship of the administrators. The Players Association can play a similar role in England.

These on-the-field incidents have certainly proliferated over the last twenty years or so. Each in its own way seems rather trivial in retrospect: John Snow's barging into Gavaskar at Lord's in 1971, Geoffrey Boycott's bat throwing in Australia, Holding and others kicking over the stumps, Dennis Lillee's aluminium bat incident – all undesirable but not individually worth too much fuss. More recently, however, some of the scenes have become a little uglier – the Miandad/Lillee showdown was not pleasant, nor are the reports of swearing at and intimidating umpires. While the so-called 'sledging' of batsmen by close fielders has been practised at all levels for years, it is perhaps more concentrated now. It is not simply caused by the money, though, since the practice is imitated with tremendous vehemence in club and league cricket. The abuse of umpires must be of questionable use anyway. In the older days the canny professional was more likely to get the umpire on his side with psychology and flattery, than to openly annoy him with swearing and abuse.

Disciplinary actions by the game's ruling bodies have, as we have noted, been muted by the fear of legal action. Nevertheless, there has been a steady increase in the number of suspensions and fines, not as extensive as the soccer system but heading in that direction. Snow was suspended for one game after the Gavaskar incident. Ian Chappell received a three-week suspension in 1980 for swearing at an umpire. This was the first such action by the ACB but has been followed by others. Tony Greig was twice in trouble for remarks he made in newspapers. Initially he was severely reprimanded and the second offence brought a two-month TCCB suspension. Chris Old was the centre of a similar case in 1983 when a £2000 fine was coupled with suspension. Both tennis and soccer have a points system followed by automatic punishment, and cricket may have to follow suit.

The incidents regarding betting on matches by players have already been mentioned and they have brought punishments of varying degree. Perhaps the most potentially dangerous disciplinary issue that could arise concerns the use of drugs by players. There were accusations surrounding the England tour to New Zealand in 1983/4 which were found to be groundless but should not be ignored. In the USA a rapidly increasing number of leading football and baseball players have been suspended and sent on rehabilitation courses. Some, including famous names, have even been imprisoned. Another form of drug-taking is designed to improve performance and this could one day be transferred from athletics to cricket. A fast bowler, particularly in a one-day game, could get significant benefit from a short-lived, energy-producing drug. While this may seem far-fetched in the world of cricket, if that is the way society is moving then the game will not be immune.

Perhaps the most controversial example of player suspension in recent years, however, has been the three-year ban imposed on Gooch and his rebel South African tourists. This brings us to perhaps the most significant controversy of modern cricket. The more recent events regarding South Africa and her relations with the rest of the cricket world have been recounted so many times in cricket books over the last decade and a half that it would be tedious to repeat it all here. For detailed accounts of the d'Oliveira affair, the 'Stop the Seventy Tour' campaign, the political manoeuvrings of South African cricket administrators (both white and non-white), and the more recent rebel tours, one should turn to *Wisden, Barclays World of Cricket*, the autobiographies of such as Swanton, Cowdrey and d'Oliveira himself, and the books cited in the bibliography by Moorhouse, Rait Kerr and Peebles, Hain, Birley and, indeed, a host of others. Debate of the various issues has been characterized by extreme polarization. On this, more than any other cricket topic, people tend to line up either violently for or against. Such a deeply felt split of opinion is typical of political subjects and neatly reinforces the basic thesis of this book that cricket is an integral part of everyday life and is shaped and influenced by the same forces that shape society as a whole.

During the period up to the late seventies the issue was a relatively straightforward one. South Africa practised racial discrimination *in sport*, and this basic fact was sufficient for a great many people to urge non-contact as a matter of principle. The most important ethic in sport – that human relations are improved and facilitated – was being injured. In this sense their behaviour has been similar to that of Nazi Germany where world-class Jewish athletes were kept out of national teams. This racial segregation in sports does not happen in many other regimes, however poor their human rights records. The decision to ostracize South Africa was, therefore, one of principle rather than simply a tactical move to put pressure on a political regime that appeared distasteful. At that time the main opposing view – apart from a tiny minority who supported the South African policies – was that continued sporting ties could be used to encourage change from within. This was the so-called 'bridge building' idea. It is probably fair to say that this latter view was the majority opinion of people within the cricket and rugby worlds, and that ostracizing was urged most strongly by people with no special interest in sport. Nevertheless, the move for breaking with South Africa won the day as cricket was joined by rugby, the Olympics, tennis and gymnastics in a total ban on sporting involvement. Later, the less prominent sports like hockey, squash, snooker and netball joined the list.

During the eighties, however, the picture has become a more complicated one. The sporting world had laid down the condition for South Africa's re-entry into international competition as a complete removal of segregation in domestic sport. Cricket has largely achieved this and South Africa can point to mixed clubs, black players in the Currie Cup and now the successful West Indian tours. In addition, many English county players are providing coaching for African children under the sponsorship of companies like Barclays. There are, however, several barriers to a simple resumption of sporting links. Most importantly, the non-white Test playing countries – the West Indies, India, Pakistan and Sri Lanka – have made it clear that any such resumption could lead to a total split in the cricket world, as they would be unwilling to play against any country with official sporting links to South Africa. This view is in harmony with the hard-line group within the black South African cricket organizations whose motto is 'No normal cricket in an abnormal society'. Their point is that the racial mixing within cricket is rendered false and superficial by the fact that a black player immediately becomes 'inferior' and discriminated against as soon as he leaves the cricket ground. Cricket is one of the few areas of South African life that is changing. Conversely, those who support a resumption of sporting links – both within South Africa and abroad – are left speechless with frustration since they can point to the fact that all the original criteria have been met. In addition, they argue that many of the non-white cricket playing countries have poor civil/racial rights records of their own, and are in no position to take a 'holier than thou' stance.

If anything, the issue seems to be even more political than it was originally. When Mrs Thatcher urged withdrawal from the Moscow Olympics in 1980 it was because of the West's disgust at the invasion of Afghanistan and of Russia's unsavoury domestic and foreign policies. While not condoning Russia's actions, many felt this was a calculating use of athletics for political purposes in an issue totally separate from sport. It appeared at odds with the view of many in the Conservative government that a ban on playing sport with South Africa was a restriction of personal freedom and constituted an undesirable mixing of politics and sport. The apparent difference in rules when dealing with a communist regime and an extreme right-wing one was commented on by many. Even within political parties there is considerable dissension on the issue. The Minister of Sport, Neil Macfarlane, in opposing the recent England rugby tour to South Africa, said, 'I believe apartheid offends the very ethic of sport, which is supposed to embrace freedom, fairness and social contact.' Others feel that the rights of individual players or associations to play wherever they wish should not be endangered by government.

To summarize, cricket has certainly reflected and been influenced by the social conditions in South Africa, to put it mildly! Cricket is, however, only one small part in the greater debate over South Africa. Here, as so often, many cricket enthusiasts tend to lose a sense of proportion concerning the greater world outside the game. It often seems that the curtailment of the Test Match careers of players like Pollock, Richards, Rice and Procter is viewed as a far sadder and more weighty issue than the cold-blooded and remorseless denial of education and basic human rights to an entire nation.

The softening of racialism in the area of sport, while it does not impress the hard-line black activists, may in reality be the start of a major improvement in other walks of life. A parallel can be found in America where the black athlete was accepted and even adulated by the white public long before racialist laws and customs were revoked in the country at large. If this scenario is played out in South Africa – admittedly a far more extreme problem – then the sporting ban of the seventies and eighties will have done inestimable social good. The question which will remain is the precise timing of a resumption of 'normal' relations so that progress is not halted.

While it is unfortunate to finish this book on such an emotive and controversial issue as the South African problem, it is perhaps appropriate. If any trend has dominated the post-war sporting scene, including cricket, it is the steady increase in controversy, argument and dissatisfaction. The days are gone when the spectator could relish an unchanging game, the players knew their place and the subject of money was hardly a factor. As in life, those days are long gone. It is fascinating to speculate on the contents of an updated version of this book in the year 2000. The game may be unrecognizable but two points can be made with some certainty. Firstly, the seeds for those changes have already been sown, and secondly, the nature of the game will be dictated by the society in which it is played.

Bibliography

A great many published sources were used in the preparation of this book. Those listed below were the most useful or are quoted in the text. In addition, much was obtained from a variety of county yearbooks and histories, biographies and tour books.

Altham, H. S. *et al, Hampshire County Cricket* (Phoenix, 1957)

Altham, H. S., Swanton, E. W., *A History of Cricket* (Allen & Unwin, 1962)

Arlott, J., Most of his published books were referred to but of particular use were: *Concerning Cricket* (Longmans, 1949); *Fred. Portrait of a Fast Bowler* (Eyre & Spottiswoode, 1972); *The Echoing Green* (Longmans, 1952); *The Picture of Cricket* (Penguin, 1955); *Vintage Summer: 1947* (Eyre & Spottiswoode, 1967)

Bannister, A., *Cricket Cauldron* (Stanley Paul, 1954)

Barker, R. S., *The Cricketing Family Edrich* (Pelham, 1976)

Barnes, S. G., *It Isn't Cricket* (Collins, 1953)

Birley, D., *The Willow Wand* (Macdonald & Janes, 1979)

Blofeld, H., *The Packer Affair* (Collins, 1978)

Bowen, R., *Cricket. A History* (Eyre & Spottiswoode, 1970)

Bowen, R. (Editor), *Cricket Quarterly 1963-70*

Brookes, C., *English Cricket. The Game and Its Players Through The Ages* (Weidenfeld & Nicolson, 1978)

Cardus, N., Many of his books but notably: *English Cricket* (Collins, 1945)

Caro, A., *With a Straight Bat* (Hong Kong, 1979)

Compton, D. C. S., *End of an Innings* (Oldbourne, 1958)

Cowdrey, M. C., *MCC. The Autobiography of a Cricketer* (Hodder & Stoughton, 1976)

Cricketer, The

D'Oliveira, B. L., *Time to Declare* (Dent, 1980)

Dollery, H. E., *Professional Captain* (Stanley Paul, 1952)

Ellacott, S. E., *A History of Everyday Things in England, Vol. V, 1904-68* (Batsford, 1968)

Evans, T. G., *The Gloves Are Off* (Hodder & Stoughton, 1960)

Fingleton, J., Information has been gleaned from all Fingleton's books of reminiscence and tour descriptions.

Ford, J., *Cricket. A Social History 1700-1835* (David & Charles, 1972)

Frith, D., *The Golden Age of Cricket 1890-1914* (Lutterworth, 1978)

Girouard, M., *The Return to Camelot. Chivalry and the English Gentleman* (Yale University Press, 1981)

Green, Brig. M. A., *Sporting Campaigner* (Stanley Paul, 1956)
Gregg, P., *The Welfare State* (Harrap, 1967)

Hain, P., 'The Politics of Sport and Apartheid', Chapter 10 in *Sport, Culture and Ideology* Edited by J. Hargreaves (Routledge & Kegan Paul, 1982)
Harris, H. A., *Sport in Britain* (Stanley Paul, 1975)
Hopkins, H., *The New Look: A Social History of the Forties and Fifties in Britain* (Houghton Mifflin, 1964)

Inglis, F., *The Name of the Game* (Heinemann, 1977)
Insole, D., *Cricket from the Middle* (Heinemann, 1960)

James, C. L. R., *Beyond a Boundary* (Hutchinson, 1963)
Johnson, W. *et al.*, *A Short Economic and Social History of Twentieth-Century Britain* (Allen & Unwin, 1967)

Kay, J., *A History of County Cricket. Lancashire* (Barker, 1972)
Kilburn, J. M., *Overthrows* (Stanley Paul, 1975); *Thanks to Cricket* (Stanley Paul, 1972)

Laker, J., *Over To Me* (Muller, 1960)

Martin-Jenkins, C., *The Complete Who's Who of Test Match Cricketers* (Orbis, 1978)
Marwick, A., *British Society Since 1945* (Penguin, 1982)
McFarlane, P., *A Game Divided* (Hutchinson, 1977)
Moorhouse, G., *Lord's* (Hodder & Stoughton, 1983)
Morrah, P., *The Golden Age of Cricket* (Eyre & Spottiswoode, 1967)

Pollard, J., *Australian Cricket. The Game and the Players* (Hodder & Stoughton, 1983)
Pycroft, Rev. J., *The Cricket Field* (St James' Press, 1922)

Rait Kerr, D., Peebles, I., *Lord's 1946-70* (Harrap, 1971)
Robinson, R., *Between Wickets* (Collins, 1948); *From the Boundary* (Collins, 1951)

Sheppard, Rev. D. S., *Parson's Pitch* (Hodder & Stoughton, 1964)
Sillitoe, A. E., *Britain in Figures. A Handbook of Social Statistics* (Penguin, 1971)
Sloane, P. J., *Sport in the Market?* (Institute of Economic Affairs, 1980)
Statham, J. B., *Cricket Merry-go-round* (Stanley Paul, 1956)
Stern, W. M., *Britain Yesterday and Today* (Longmans, 1969)
Strutt, J., *The Sports and Pastimes of the People of England* (London, 1810)
Swanton, E. W., *Follow On* (Collins, 1977); *Sort of a Cricket Person* (Collins, 1972)
Swanton, E. W. (Editor), *Barclays World of Cricket* (Collins, 1980)
The Times
Trollope, A., *The Fixed Period*
Tyson, F., *A Typhoon Called Tyson* (Heinemann, 1961)

White, D., 'Is County Cricket Dying?' Article in *New Society* 22 June, 1978
Wisden Cricket Monthly
Wisden Cricketer's Almanack
Wooller, W., *A History of County Cricket. Glamorgan* (Barker, 1971)

Index